LULLABY QUILTS

for Babies and Dolls

by Margaret Boyles

MEREDITH PRESS®

NEW YORK

DEAR QUILTER:

Creating beauty is surely one of the most satisfying experiences. The joy we felt as this book took shape was enhanced by working with a superb artist, designer, and teacher—Margaret Boyles. Her unique style shines in every drawing, and her use of color and texture brings new meaning to classic motifs. Most of all, she has been a gracious mentor and friend.

We at Meredith® Press are very proud of the craft books we publish. They are of the highest quality and offer projects for every level of crafting skill. Meredith® Press books feature large, full-color photographs of all projects, as well as instructions and charts that are simple and readable.

We hope you find as much satisfaction and pleasure in using *Lullaby Quilts for Babies and Dolls* as we have had in bringing this book to you.

Sincerely,

Mary Williams   *Guido Anderau*

Mary Williams and Guido Anderau

Meredith® Press is an imprint of *Meredith® Books*
President, Book Group: Joseph J. Ward
Vice President and Editorial Director: Elizabeth P. Rice

For Meredith® Press
Executive Editor: Maryanne Bannon
Editorial Project Managers: Mary Williams, Guido Anderau
Production Manager: Bill Rose
Copy Editor: Sydney Matus
Book Designer: Ulrich Ruchti
Photography and Illustrations: Margaret Boyles
Cover Photography: Perry Struse

TABLE OF CONTENTS

A NOTE FROM THE AUTHOR

Sarah Miller James was a lady I should have liked to know. There are pictures of her with her wonderful white hair piled high and wearing the prim Victorian shirtwaists and long skirts of her days, things in my home that she made reminding me of her every day. Yet though she was one of my maternal great-grandmothers, I never saw her. I know from family stories that she had a wonderful sense of humor, a bubbling laugh, and that there was a trace of impishness behind that proper Victorian pose.

One of the things I have always liked most about her was her love of fine needlework, for among my family treasures are some of her works. There is a fine wool coverlet which family stories say she wove as a little girl during the Civil War, while her father and brothers were gone to war. Its pale yellow color and striped borders came from plants she used for dyes, and its soft wool is especially fine. But the piece I love most is a little quilt she made for my grandfather in the months before he was born. Apparently she made one for each of her children in a size to fit a trundle bed. My grandfather's is in excellent condition, despite its having been made around the time of his birth in 1886. Naturally, it is cotton, off-white with a wonderful pieced design in tan and red calico. The quilting is geometric and in very close, finely stitched rows, the pieced design in a small size suitable for a child's quilt.

It was used every day until my grandfather grew so tall he needed a longer bed; then it was folded across the foot of a bed as a throw. I remember it always being somewhere on a bed in my grandparents' home. Then, one fortunate day, it came to reside in my home, where we enjoy its quiet beauty and treasure the memories it holds.

I think the quilt and the tradition Sarah James established in making a quilt for each baby in the time before it was born inspired me to try to follow that path. I remember buying the kit for my first attempt. The display was a finished quilt—white, pink, and gray. It was an appliqué pattern in the design of a pussy willow tree. The blossoms were baby kittens curled up in the cups of the flowers. I was enchanted and started immediately.

Glenn was born before the appliqué was finished, so the little quilt went into a drawer. Then when the second and third babies were coming, I worked on it again, finally finishing the quilting for the fourth baby. And it was just as adorable as the model quilt had been in the store. Maybe the delays were some kind of providence, for Baby Hope adopted the quilt as her "blankie" and wore the poor little thing to shreds carrying it with her everywhere.

I have thought about those two little quilts many times during the writing and designing that went into this book, and tried to make small treasures that you will enjoy making and that someone else will love and cherish for many years. I still haven't decided if I would prefer my quilts to survive only slightly worn or to be loved into oblivion like the pussy willows! I do know that I am an incurable romantic who puts love into every stitch, and I hope that the little one who snuggles into one of my quilts can feel the love that is so much a part of the real warmth in any hand-made quilt.

And so I have included a range of my favorite designs for you to make—the cloud-soft romantic Bébé, the bright Rainbow, the exuberant Celebration, and, my very favorite, Irish Lullaby—hoping you will find many joys stitching them. If you have never quilted, there are easy designs that will inspire you to make some of the more intricate ones or perhaps a full-size quilt. If there is no baby in your life, or if you have an antique or country-inspired decorating scheme, one of these little quilts "antiqued" with tea might add just the right touch of softness over a sofa or hung by the door.

Since doll quilts have become one of the most sought after collectibles, and as they are so much fun to make, a collection of tiny quilts is also included. These, too, are wonderful "antiqued" and hung as accents. The doll quilts range from quick-and-easy stenciled delights like Bluebirds for Baby to heavily quilted Little Star to traditional Postage Stamp Stripe to shadow-embroidered Petite Bébé. You'll find your own favorite quickly, and very soon some lucky little girl will be able to tuck her baby doll into its cradle with her own little quilt.

As I finish, I want to wish you all the pleasures to be found in quilting. It is not an accident that this art has always been America's most favored form of needlework. There is some special chemistry that takes place when enjoyable stitchery can combine with utility to make something that will be so loved and cherished. A quilt has all those properties, and I hope this book will be the one that introduces you to those pleasures.

THE BASICS

MATERIALS

The best advice about quilting ever given me was to use the best materials I could find and afford, and to do my best work always. Then, my grandmother assured me, I would always finish with a quilt I could use with pride and enjoyment throughout its long life. Those words spoken so matter-of-factly many years ago are still part of my quilting philosophy, for they are just as true today as they were then.

Most forms of needlework are easier when the quality of the materials is fine. This is especially true of quilting. Fabric that is too thick, uneven, or loosely woven is much more difficult to cut, piece, and quilt than a wonderful soft, tightly woven cotton. Quilters love fabrics, collecting not only beautiful and intriguing prints and colors, but also those that yield interesting texture and quilting ease.

To make duplication of the quilts in this book easy, a Materials list at the beginning of each instruction details the fabrics used. In addition another section—Finding the Materials—discusses the fiber content, the prints and colors, and any changes that can be made without making a great difference in the finished look of the quilt. The tips in this section are very helpful.

Fabrics

The best source for the cotton quilt fabrics is a store or mail order catalog that specializes in quilting materials. Since these are usually operated by quilters, the stock is chosen and displayed to appeal to quilters and to help with selecting fabrics for a project. This one-stop source is also the best place to find the right batting, thread, and—most important—advice.

Cotton has always been the preferred fiber for quilting. It is easy to cut, sew, and press. In addition, it wears well, withstanding much washing and rough handling. When the time needed to make a quilt is considered, one naturally seeks a fabric that will make a beautiful quilt that will last "forever."

The quality of a cotton fabric is largely determined by the thread count. Choose those that are tightly woven, so they do not fray when cut and so the batting won't migrate through when the quilt is used. Most of these quilting cottons are referred to as being 45 inches wide, but in truth the width varies from 42 to 45 inches. To be consistent and to avoid shortages, the requirements in this book are based on the 42-inch width, unless only a wider piece will do (and that will then be specified). If your fabric happens to be 45 inches wide, you may have a small surplus, but it will not be enough to warrant cutting back on the yardage specified.

All fabrics to be used in a quilt should be washed before construction to remove the sizing and to ensure that any possible shrinkage will occur *before* the pieces are cut. This washing does not need be a full cycle in the machine with detergent. Usually just a minute of agitation with a small amount of detergent, followed by a thorough rinse, is sufficient. A whirl in the dryer should be enough to finish.

Small pieces of fabric can be taken directly from the washing machine and ironed to dry. Do not use starch unless the fabric has lost all its body and would be difficult to handle without it. In this case spray-on sizing is usually a good choice for restoring the original finish.

Check dark colors—especially reds—for colorfastness. Dampen a suspect piece and leave it on a white towel for a few minutes to see if it will bleed. If it does, soak it several hours in cold water to which vinegar and salt have been added. Rinse until the water is clear, then dry it on a white towel to check again for bleeding. If you are not sure it is safe, discard it.

Some of the more delicate quilts in this book have been made from a very fine Swiss batiste that is used primarily for clothing, especially "heirloom sewing." It is a very durable, soft, smooth cotton that has a subtle sheen. These elegant little quilts are true heirlooms that are made to be very special gifts, because the fabric, lace, and design will last for generations and eventually become part of the baby's heritage.

It is possible in many cases to substitute a good-quality poly-cotton blend batiste for the Swiss in the heirloom quilts and thereby decrease the cost of materials by about half. The difference in the outward appearance will be small, but if your aim is to make a very special gift that you know will endure, do use the Swiss. The best place to find both batiste fabrics is a shop specializing in smocking and heirloom supplies.

Some laces and eyelet embroideries have also been used on the little quilts. Although not usually thought of as quilting materials, they are natural additions for making delicate little nursery accessories.

When the Materials list specifies 100 percent cotton lace edging, the lace is usually an imported one found easily where heirloom sewing supplies are sold. Some of these laces are now being made with 10 percent nylon added for extra strength. This is usually a fine thread that attaches the motif to the background netting and does not alter the delicate appearance. Domestic and nylon laces may be substituted for the cotton ones, if you prefer.

Eyelet-embroidered edging can be the imported on Swiss batiste or more easily found cotton. Choose edging with a width, pattern, and fabric appropriate for the quilt.

Batting

Although it is completely hidden, the batting has almost as much effect on a quilt's final appearance as the color and outer fabrics. Some battings allow for the tiny stitches of yesterday, while others are fluffy and thick; some shrink just a bit to suggest the quilt is old; some are warmer than others. Each adds its own signature to the finished whole.

There are many different batting products available. Some are the natural fibers—cotton, wool, or silk—while many are all-synthetic or a blend of natural and man-made. For the baby and doll quilts included in this book, only a few of these choices have been used, but the following brief discussion will be helpful if the exact batting used in a specific quilt cannot be found.

You will notice that in the Materials list for each quilt a specific weight and fiber batting is noted. This is so you can duplicate the pictured finished quilt. Sometimes another weight batting will work nicely without altering the final product too much, but other times it will alter the basic structure of the quilt. For instance, if Simplicity on page 30 were to be made with a low-loft batting, it would lose the wonderful puffy feel that contributes so much to the loveliness of such a simple design.

Batting for quilts is available in standard crib, twin, full, queen, and king sizes. There is also a choice of loft—in order of thickness: fleece, low-loft, medium-loft, and high-loft. Manufacturers sometimes give battings other names, like "traditional" and "classic," but usually add a note describing the loft to avoid confusion.

• Cotton. Quilt batting from this wonderful natural material has been made by basically the same process for hundreds of years. It is an especially good choice for a little quilt that will probably get a lot of hard wear. It is not quite as warm as batting of wool or polyester, but that is often an advantage.

When cotton batting is washed, it shrinks by almost the same percentage as cotton fabrics shrink in the first washing. Therefore, it is a good idea to eliminate the prewashing of the cotton covering fabrics and allow all the shrinkage to take place at once, after the quilt has been finished. This shrinkage imparts an unmistakable, lovely old appearance to a quilt. You can see the very slight puckering it imparts at the seams and quilting lines in Patched Hearts on page 107 and Celebration on page 35.

Most quilters find the cotton batting more difficult to hand-stitch, so prefer to use it when machine-quilting, which is where it really shines.

• Cotton and polyester. This newer batting, made from a blend of cotton and polyester, benefits from the best properties of both fibers. It imparts the same old look that all-cotton adds, but is as lightweight and comfortable as polyester. It is easier to hand-quilt than all-cotton and excellent for machine work.

• Wool. This wonderfully warm batting is a specialty item, but can usually be found in quilt shops or ordered from mail order sources. Like anything else made from wool, it needs special care, but is so luxurious it is worth it. I have found much more use of wool batting in Australia and New Zealand, where the sheep industry is very important, but its traditional use continues here in America.

Wool batting makes a warm, soft quilt. The batting is easily stitched either by hand or machine. Most makers of wool batting suggest dry cleaning for quilts containing this filler, but if care is taken, these can be hand-washed like a fine sweater.

• Silk. Now, this is really luxury! Usually imported from Japan, where the silk industry flourishes, these battings are very soft and warm—and, not unexpectedly, expensive. A quilt finished with this fiber batting can be quilted by hand or machine with ease.

• Polyester or synthetic fibers. Man-made fibers have greatly changed our lives in recent years, and most quilters believe polyester batting is one of the best products of this fiber innovation. The manufacturing process allows a wide range of thickness, or loft, giving us many choices for the basic characteristics of our quilts. When shopping, buy only major brand-name batting packaged and labeled for quilting. Many of the others are intended for other craft uses and will not perform well in a quilt.

Most of the packaged polyester battings have a coating on the outside of the fluffed inner mass that is designed to hold the batting together and prevent the fibers from migrating—bunching up—and also from working their way through the outer fabric to make an unsightly mess called "bearding." Even so, these two annoyances sometimes happen. To avoid the latter, choose tightly woven fabrics for the quilt top. Migrating usually can be prevented by spacing the quilting stitches close enough to prevent shifting.

Thread

The thread used is one of those little details that can make a quilt a pleasant or a difficult project, an enduring treasure or a short-lived disappointment. If it snarls or breaks frequently, the piecing and the quilting are onerous tasks rather than fun. If it is not strong enough, the seams come apart or the quilting stitches break. If it is too strong, it will cut the fabric; too heavy and it spoils the stitches.

For these little quilts I have used 100 percent cotton mercerized thread exclusively. Mercerization is a chemical treatment that makes thread very smooth and strong, thus good for hand or machine work. Cotton is best for both piecing and quilting because, when the seams are pressed, the stitches flatten and seem to become part of the fabric rather than remaining a row of little loops sitting on the surface, as happens with cotton-covered synthetic or all-synthetic threads. Fifty weight (#50) is a good choice for sewing most of the cottons when joining pieces and blocks or adding binding. It is also a good thread for quilting on these small projects because it allows you to make beautiful small stitches.

Unless the fabric colors are all dark, off-white or ecru thread is usually the best color for piecing and construction. It is rarely visible in seams, even when a great many colors are combined.

Many manufacturers make a special thread for quilting. It is most always cotton, but it is a heavy weight and has a wax coating. Most of these threads are very good, but not appropriate for the little quilts.

A new presence in the quilting thread category is a fine transparent nylon. This is very pretty for machine quilting. The thread seems to disappear into the fabric, leaving only the texture and pattern of the quilting. It has been used for the machine quilting on the Rainbow quilt on page 94 and on several others. You can see the textured results in the photographs. Use this thread for machine quilting, but *not* for piecing or construction.

Check first for this thread in a quilt shop to be certain of buying nylon meant for quilting. Locating it can be frustrating, because the reel is simply wrapped in a plastic sleeve and not labeled as quilting thread, but you will recognize it, as it is usually wound on a 3-inch cardboard cylinder instead of a conventional spool. It is a fine, soft thread, not the wiry utility nylon thread of past years. There are both clear and smoky gray colors. Use the gray on dark colors, the clear on all others.

It is possible to machine-quilt with the nylon as the top thread of the machine and a cotton thread on the bobbin, if desired. Since most sewing machines are very precisely adjusted, make a sample to be sure the difference in the weights of the threads won't cause an unbalanced stitch. You will know this is happening if you see the bobbin thread pulling through to the top, or vice versa.

Needles

Needles—another of the little things that mean a great deal more than their size would indicate! My grandmother always had one favorite needle that she used, until it became so corroded it couldn't penetrate the fabric easily, or until it broke! It was bent into a slight curve from so much use, but she would rub it in and out of her strawberry emery cushion and keep going until she had no choice but to break in a new one. This must have been the result of growing up in a small southern town in Victorian times, when it was not so easy to come by a needle, or perhaps a thriftiness developed in the Great Depression. While I treasure the memories of her fussing with her needle, I nevertheless enjoy a shiny new needle that glides in and out effortlessly and always recommend using new needles as often as needed.

Keep a supply of needles on hand. Many quilters use a needle called a between, or quilting needle. It is a short needle with a small round eye. A size 11 is average. But if you buy a package of assorted sizes, you might try a larger size 10 or a smaller 12 to see which helps you make the most even stitches.

Even though the between is the accepted needle for quilting, any needle that enables you to make the prettiest stitches is fine. Many quilters are surprised to learn that my favored hand-quilting needle is a size 10 crewel. Most often used for fine embroidery, this needle is a little longer than the between and has an elongated eye.

The needle should make an opening in the fabric large enough to allow the thread to pass through without excessive abrasion. Then the hole should close up. If the needle is too fine, the thread will constantly wear thin. If it is too thick, it will be clumsy to handle and the openings made may remain visible.

Sewing machine needles are as important as hand-sewing needles. For piecing and construction, use a size 80 needle, which is a utility size and compatible with #50 thread. For the machine quilting on these little quilts, the same needle can be used. Change needles after about eight hours of sewing, even if they seem to be working fine. Sometimes little burrs form and weaken the threads. Since it is hoped that your quilts will last several generations, no step as simple as changing the needle should be skipped.

Basic Sewing Supplies

If you already own a sewing machine, you probably already have accumulated most of the basic sewing supplies listed in the box.

Sewing Machines

Quilting does not require a fancy new sewing machine. You can piece and do decorative machine quilting as long as your machine makes a good, even straight stitch and the tension is adjustable. One necessity is a walking or quilting foot, which can be bought for most machines. This attachment feeds the fabric from the top layer of a quilt through at the same rate as the feed dogs carry through the bottom layer, avoiding puckering and shifting problems.

If you wish to do machine appliqué, the machine must be able to do a zigzag stitch.

On the other hand, the new machines are wonders! Beautiful and quiet, computer-controlled or mechanical, they make any sewing pure pleasure. All have a wide array of attachments and specialized presser feet; one even has a built-in dual-feed device for quilting!

Scissors

Construction of a quilt requires at least two pairs of sharp, well-maintained scissors. A good pair of 8- or 9-inch shears is necessary for cutting fabric, batting, bias strips, etc. In addition, a small pair of embroidery scissors is needed for snipping ends of quilting threads.

Pins

Sharply pointed straight pins a little longer than the standard silk pins are a necessity when pinning the layers of a quilt together, but you'll like them so much you'll find them replacing the older pins you have been using for ordinary sewing. Buy ones with a glass head so you won't have to worry about melting them with the iron.

If you are careful, some of the small quilts that follow can be pinned and machine-quilted without basting. To avoid rusting and other discolorations

Basic Sewing Supplies
Basting thread
Sewing machine thread to match the fabric of your project in a weight indicated in the Materials list
Scissors
Assorted hand-sewing needles
Assorted machine needles
Pins
Marking pens and pencils
Tape measure, ruler, or straightedge

the pins may cause, buy nickel-plated safety pins about an inch long. This size has sharp enough points to penetrate the three layers of the quilt without leaving holes.

Pressing Equipment

For most sewers, a good iron is almost as critical to a well-made finished project as the sewing machine, and that is especially true when quilting. Each seam should be pressed after it is sewn, and when working with cottons it is best if the iron is one with adjustable heat settings and produces enough steam to do a good job. These requirements are met by most household irons.

Several of the European sewing machine producers have revived the small household version of the industrial-type presses. If you have one, you will find it very useful for pressing seams in the quilting process, as multiple pieces can be individually finger-pressed then laid on the press to be ironed together, all at once.

An ironing board cover marked into 1-inch grids can also be a very big help when pressing. If it is installed with the grid perfectly straight and you line up the edges of the quilt piece with the grid, it is unlikely that the piece will be distorted by pressing. If a printed cover is not easily available, a viable substitute can be made by wrapping the board in a piece of 1-inch gingham.

Basic Quilting Supplies

A trip to a quilt shop acquaints one with an almost bewildering array of new tools and gadgets to make quiltmaking easier and more nearly perfect. For the little quilts, few of these are necessary, but shopping around while planning more quilts is certainly fun!

Marking Tools

Marking a quilt top for quilting has always been the job we wished we could forget, not because it is such a terrible task, but because there are so many markers and so many opinions about which to use. The traditional tool is a #4H lead pencil, which makes a fine line that can usually be removed easily either with a fabric eraser or by washing.

The washout pen and pencil are very helpful tools for the quiltmaker, but they must be used with caution. The pen is very easy to use and quickly makes lines that are readily followed. There are several brands. Buy one and test it. Draw on the actual fabric of the quilt. Then rinse the fabric to determine if the markings really will wash away. Check to see if it comes back after the fabric has dried.

Try never to touch a washout pen line with the iron, as this sets some permanently. Use the pen sparingly. Instead of drawing a line, make a series of small light dots. When you finish the quilt top, either submerge the piece or run water through it to remove the chemicals.

Basic Quilting Supplies

Quilting needles
A walking or dual-feed presser
    foot for the sewing machine
Quilting thread as noted in
    Materials lists
Batting
Rotary cutter and mat
Draftsman's right triangle

Avoid the disappearing ink pens. The purple color will usually disappear within twenty-four hours, but the chemical remains in the fabric and there is no history yet to indicate the effect this might have on the life of the fabric.

There are many more markers suitable for marking a quilt. The best advice is to suggest that every one be tested on the fabric of each quilt before it is used. Then use as few markings as possible when setting up a design. Sometimes a fold will establish a line as well as a pen. Other times—as for Little Lambs (page 112)—only a dot marks the corners of the squares, while the stencil itself establishes the outlines.

Special Cutting Tools

Among the new tools that you might not have but should think about are the rotary cutter and mat and their companion ruler.

The rotary cutter is really a simple little tool that cuts smooth edges through multiple layers of fabric. This is a set that can save many hours of marking and cutting pieces. For the purposes in this book, buy the smaller cutter, a mat about 18 by 22 inches, and a wide ruler with a lip at one end. The markings on the ruler and the mat make it possible to cut many small pieces perfectly in a very short time. This set is a very worthwhile investment if you intend to make several quilts.

Books and Magazines

Quilters laugh at themselves for their collecting habits. We all want a huge "library" of fabrics and to own every tool invented. And, all of us collect books and magazines avidly. Actually, these are all excellent investments—especially when the inspiration for a quilt hits at midnight, or later!

New quilters should check books often. There are many well-written instruction manuals that are very helpful. Most have been written by experienced teachers who have developed original techniques and share them generously. Many are books of designs and variations of a theme and should be purchased when one particular quilt is what you wish to make. Others are less-impressive-looking little volumes that nevertheless contain a wealth of good information. Some are primers on rotary cutting, speed cutting, strip piecing, or machine quilting. There is even a dictionary of quilting terms, and a manual that can be very helpful in improving your hand-quilting stitch. These are very good investments and should be added to your library.

Quilter's magazines are a source of inspiration and will offer not only quilting tips and instructions but also new and innovative ideas. Treat yourself to one or subscribe. You'll find hours of enjoyment just reading about quilts and how to make them, and also learn about other quilters, their stitching problems, and their solutions. We may laugh about our collections, but they are very absorbing and useful.

QUILTING BASICS

Getting Started

A little quilt is an excellent introduction to quiltmaking in general. For the most part, the processes involved are the same as those needed to complete a large quilt, but the materials are less costly and the time needed is much shorter. One has all the same wonderful experiences in a smaller package and is ready to begin another quilt—either large or small—immediately.

If you are completely new to quiltmaking, you might want to begin with Simplicity (page 30), which was designed both as a beginner's project and to answer pleas from several new mothers who did not want to add one more cartoon character, clown, or cute baby animal to their nursery. Making the quilt necessitates buying 3½ yards of fabric, a crib-size batting, and the quilting presser foot for the machine if your machine is not equipped with dual feed. For this small investment, when the project has been finished you will have moved through the basics of cutting, layering and basting, machine quilting, and finishing with a corded piping. Add a new technique with each successive quilt and a quiltmaker is born.

If you decide to make a traditional pieced quilt like Lucky Stars (page 82), begin by cutting and making one square to determine that you enjoy the technique used. Before buying all the fabrics needed, have some fun trying out the design. Buy fat quarters of the colors you think you want to use. Cut the pieces for one or two stars and follow the instructions to stitch several blocks. The construction methods given are variations of some new methods of making the blocks. They are faster and more accurate than the traditional methods. (I well remember the first Ohio Star I stitched as a young quilter. Those bias edges were a nightmare, and I decided I would only work on grain forevermore. My nine-year-old granddaughter's experience was very different when she stitched her first square and found all the points perfect. Her little blue and white quilt peeks out from the shelf of an armoire filled with quilts.)

If stitching the sample squares convinces you it would be enjoyable to piece enough for a crib quilt, purchase additional fabrics and begin work. The squares you have already finished can be incorporated into the quilt or made up into pillows.

Similarly, if you decide to stencil a quilt, buy a fat quarter of the cotton you would use for the quilt and the stenciling supplies needed. Cut the stencil, then lay out and paint one square. Decide if stenciling and laying out the full-size quilt is a project you would finish. After the sample is painted, set the color as directed by the manufacturer, and wash the square several times to check for colorfastness of the paints. This sample can also be finished as a pillow if you like.

Read all the material offered here and in the Materials section before starting your project. Each bit of information has been included to help make your quilting experiences a joy and the finished quilts works of love you will be proud to use or to give to lucky babies.

Fabric Preparation and Cutting

After the selected fabrics have been washed, ironed, and tested for colorfastness—see page 7—they should be trimmed to a straight edge. Do this by tearing off a small strip, pulling a thread and cutting on the line made by the removed thread, or placing a right angle on the selvage and cutting across the width of the fabric with a rotary cutter. All three methods produce a good straight beginning edge.

When the fabric is torn, the edge is very straight and exactly on grain, but there are those annoying threads coming off the edge to contend with. If the fabric is a medium to loose weave, these fraying threads can cause the loss of a fraction of an inch in the width of the pieces being torn. If this happens, compensate by stitching a slightly narrower seam or tearing a bit wider strip.

Pulling a thread in a tightly woven cotton is sometimes very time-consuming, but the resulting cut is very accurate. The thread need not be completely removed. Most of the time, even if the thread is only displaced by pulling, a line that can be used as a cutting line is made visible.

When the rotary cutter is used and the line is at a right angle to the selvage, the cut edge may be one or two threads off-grain in some spots. Since the cut is so sharp and straight, this is seldom a problem. Rotary cutting is the best and fastest method, as the edges are uniformly clean-cut and several layers of fabric can be cut at once.

Precision cutting is one of the keys to good quiltmaking, and you will find yourself combining all three methods, depending upon the project—tearing long pieces for borders and sashing, rotary cutting small shapes, and pulling threads on Swiss batiste or other delicate fibers.

In some instances, the instructions for a quilt include templates for some of the pieces. It is not necessary to use these if you cut the same size pieces using a rotary cutter. If you use the templates, carefully trace them on stencil film or cardboard. Cut them out, then draw around them on the fabric. Draw carefully so the point of the pencil stays as close as possible to the edge of the template to avoid making a piece that is too large.

When templates are used, always line up the straight edges with the vertical or horizontal grain of the fabric.

The little quilts featured in this book do not require a great deal of cutting time, detailed instructions for speed cutting, and specialized rotary cutting techniques, but if you decide to adventure into making large quilts, check some of the new books for details about these new techniques. It is amazing how applying simple twentieth-century methods can eliminate the tedium of cutting two hundred 2-inch squares that are exactly the same size and all on grain!

Accurate cutting requires a good, flat surface on which to mark and cut. Use to best advantage the grid on your dressmaking cutting board or the mat for the rotary cutter. Many times, strips and squares can be cut without a lot of painstaking marking if these aids are utilized.

When you are ready to begin cutting the pieces for your little quilt, read the Cutting Guide in the instructions and cut the largest pieces of each color first. Often this will mean cutting and setting aside the backing or border pieces first. Following these instructions will save fabric and ensure that you are able to cut all the pieces needed from the yardage specified without piecing.

Keep the pieces sorted as you cut. Usually all that is needed is to stack the little pieces as they are cut and place them by the machine. In most cases, it is not necessary to mark the pieces, but the instructions usually indicate what each piece is for and refer to the piece by that name when it is to be used.

Stitching Seams

Antique quilts are both hand-pieced and hand-quilted. For many years we thought the truly excellent quilts could only be made this way. Now we know that a machine-pieced quilt is not only faster to make, but very much stronger, and the machine stitching will not be apparent when the quilt is finished. New piecing methods make putting together even a complicated quilt top an easy, fairly quick job. Since all the little quilts in this book have been machine-pieced, completing one of these would be a good introduction to the process.

Unless specifically noted, the seam allowance for all the quilts is ¼ inch. This should be trimmed to ⅛ inch.

It is very important that the seam be stitched exactly ¼ inch from the cut edge of the fabric. Many machines have been designed so that when the right edge of the basic or utility presser foot runs along the cut edge of the fabric and the needle is in its center position, you will obtain a line of straight stitches ¼ inch from the edge. If this measurement is off by just a thread or two, the finished pieced area will not measure correctly.

To make certain your stitching is accurate, stitch two pieces of fabric in a ¼-inch seam, then measure from the cut edge to the stitching with a ruler. Check carefully—about ¼ inch is not good enough! If you need to make an adjustment and your machine has adjustable needle positions, try moving the needle. If not, place a piece of tape on the throat plate to mark a line along which to feed the pieces.

Pressing Seams

Press each seam as it is stitched. Using a steam iron and the heat setting for the fabric being used, press the seam flat. Trim the seam to ⅛ inch. Then open the stitched piece and press the seam to the darker fabric.

When pressing squares like those for the points in the Ohio Star (See Lucky Stars, page 82) patches, take care not to stretch the pieces out of their square shape. This is very easy to do when the fabric is damp from steam. To avoid stretching, line up the edges with a straight line on the ironing board and press downward without moving the iron in a pushing motion. If a piece is accidentally stretched, apply some steam and press it straight.

Sometimes it seems that getting up to iron after one seam is too much trouble. Avoid this by piecing many squares at once in assembly-line fashion, then press all at once. Some quilters set up a tabletop ironing board beside the sewing machine to speed up the process.

I do not iron my quilts after I have completed them, but I know some very important quilting teachers who do. It is a personal decision. An ironed quilt is beautifully smooth and pristine; a quilt in which the pieces are well pressed as it is constructed but which is not ironed after the quilting is complete is soft and cuddly, and the quilting much more defined.

Marking for the Quilting

In many cases, there is little or no marking for quilting required for these little quilts. Most of them are quilted around the outlines of either a stencil appliqué or a pieced design, with added stitching following inside blocks and borders. A few feature little quilted designs inside blocks and borders that must be outlined after the piecing has been completed. For the most part, the instructions direct the best time and method for making these outlines.

Read the Materials section for advice about markers and then follow the quilt's instructions. Be very careful that all your markings are removable, and test every fabric with the markers to make certain this is so. Fabrics and chemicals have ways of interacting that can surprise.

Another marking to check carefully is one that indicates placement of a stencil. The stencil paints tend to be almost transparent, allowing marks to show through. Once paint has been applied, the mark is there forever!

The instructions may suggest making a tracing of a design to retrace onto the fabric. Others might recommend making a template around which to mark. Whichever is directed is usually the easiest method for that particular project.

When I outline or trace a quilting design, I make a series of small dots instead of a solid line. Then there is less to remove later. My eye just connects the dots for me as I quilt the lines.

It is best to mark borders *after* the pieced top has been assembled and ironed. This allows for more exact placement along seam lines and accurate centering. Always begin marking a border at the center point and work toward the corners, so both ends will be alike and any small adjustment can be made at the corners.

After the quilting has been finished, remove all markings. Pencil usually comes off with a cloth eraser. The washout pens and pencils can be sponged out. If either is stubborn, immerse the quilt in water.

Assembling the Quilt

These little quilts are easy to put together—no need for a big quilting frame and several people to hold and stretch the layers to the same tension. With a little care, it is easy to layer the quilt top, batting, and backing ready for quilting.

To begin, press the top and backing well. Choose a large, clean flat surface on which to work. A table is good; many quilters use the floor if they are comfortable kneeling or crawling.

Spread the backing out flat, wrong side facing up. Onto that layer the batting, allowing it to extend about an inch beyond the backing all around. Smooth out any wrinkles. Next place the quilt top on the batting, right side up, lining up the edges with those of the backing. Make sure all three layers are straight and smoothed out.

Pin the three layers together with long straight pins, taking care not to disturb the alignment. Place the pins in horizontal rows about 3 inches apart with about 3 inches between the pins.

As you will be working without a hoop or frame, it is necessary to baste the layers together securely, so they can't shift while you are stitching. Use a good-quality white or off-white thread for basting. (When colored threads are pulled to remove them, they sometimes leave little bits of color imbedded in the fabric and batting—the darker the color, the more prominent.)

Place the basting stitches in rows 2 to 3 inches apart and baste both horizontally and vertically. Remove the pins.

If you are going to machine-quilt, it is fine to do the hand basting, but you can save some time by pinning with safety pins. (See Pins, page 11, for a description of the best kind to use.) I usually pin the layers together first with straight pins, then go back and insert the safety pins, so I can lift the quilt to fasten the pins without worrying about shifting.

Quilting

The quilting is the final touch, the touch that ties all the preceding steps together into a quilt. Whether you do it by hand or machine, this is what you have been working toward, the step most of us enjoy most.

Hand Quilting

As discussed in the Materials section, the needle and thread used are very important aspects of the quilting process. Review the information there, and experiment with different sizes and types of needles to find the one that allows you to make the smallest, most regular stitches. Think also about using a thimble. Because I make only one stitch at a time and do not need to use much pressure to push my needle through, I do not use a thimble. If you elect to gather four or five stitches on the needle before pulling it through, find a good metal thimble. Look for fairly deep depressions in the pattern of dots on the surface at the top of the thimble. These are not just ornamentation. They support the needle while you push it through the fabric.

If you have never quilted, practice on a sample made up of scraps of the batting, lining, and top fabric from your quilt. Follow the stitching instructions and enjoy making every stitch. Although the quilting stitch is the simple basic running stitch we all use for hand sewing, making it through three thick layers is a bit different from using it in a seam—not necessarily difficult, just different in the way it is made and feels.

The prettiest quilting stitches are small and the same size on the top of the quilt as on the back. Many quilters feel even size is more important than tiny stitches.

There are three entirely correct methods to achieve pretty quilting. The first is a method quilters and embroiderers call "stick and stab," in which the needle is inserted down from the top and pulled through, then reinserted from the bottom to come out again on the top. This is slow and usually not very accurate, because one has to guess where to insert the needle when it is under the quilt. A second method is worked from the top, using the underneath hand as a help to gather three or four stitches on the needle before pulling the needle through. The most even stitching is done one stitch at a time with one hand on the top, the other underneath guiding the needle. The index finger of the underneath hand can become sore from being stabbed by the needle, but can be protected with a little piece of tape or a plastic quilter's thimble.

The key to making a pretty quilting stitch is to insert the needle downward through the layers in a straight path as shown in Figure 1. On the hand above the quilt top, the needle is held between the thumb and the third finger while the index finger pushes the needle down and through until it just touches the tip of the index finger underneath.

When the finger under the quilt top feels the tip of the needle come through, it then pushes up lightly while the index finger of the hand on top pivots the needle downward until it lies on the surface of the quilt and the tip comes through to the top (Figure 2). The thread is then pulled through and the next stitch begun.

With this method and a little practice, your stitches will become very even and good speed can be developed. If you prefer to gather three or four stitches on the needle and can keep them even, use this same method, pulling

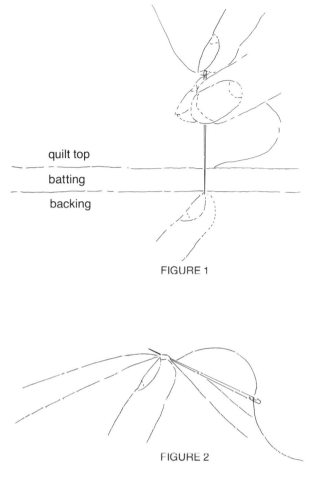

quilt top

batting

backing

FIGURE 1

FIGURE 2

the thread through when the full number of stitches has been picked up on the needle.

In the beginning, aim to make six or seven stitches per inch—counting only the stitches on the top. After a bit of practice, you will find the count is eight or nine stitches per inch. This is very pretty and a fine size for most work. The average quilter makes somewhere between eight and twelve stitches to the inch.

There will always be times when the "stick and stab" method is the only one that will work. This usually occurs when the stitching line crosses a seam line and there are multiple thicknesses of fabric or tight corners to navigate.

Stitch with an even tension, pulling the thread just enough to make the stitches lie flat on the surface, making a very slight indented line. Stitches pulled too tightly will break when the quilt is handled or stress is put on them.

Begin and end all threads with a tiny knot buried in the layers. To start a thread, make a little knot in the end of the thread. Take the thread down from the top into the batting about half an inch from where you want to start stitching, and bring the needle to the surface at that point. When the knot reaches the surface of the quilt top, give the thread a little tug or stroke the knot with your fingernail until it pops through to the inside. If that leaves a little opening still visible in the fabric, close it by pushing the threads back into place with the tip of the needle.

End a thread when there are still at least 3 inches left on the needle. Use the needle to tie a little loop knot in the thread, and pull the knot down until it is about one stitch's length from the surface of the quilt. Insert the needle at the point at which the next stitch would begin, but go down only into the batting and come to the surface about half an inch away. Pull the knot through to the inside. Cut off the thread close to the fabric. The end will disappear into the quilt.

Machine Quilting

It took quilters a long time to accept machine quilting, but the limits on our time plus new machines with dual-feed or quilting feet and new threads have inspired many to experiment with it. Several well-known quilters have elevated machine quilting to an art and have developed new methods that are both beautiful and intriguing. They have also perfected new quilting patterns that allow for continuous stitching and fewer thread ends to tie off, making this quick stitching both fun to do and fascinating.

The little quilts in this book that have been machine-quilted utilize the technique in a most basic way because they are so small. The bulk of this quilting is "stitching in the ditch," or following the outline of a block, placing the stitching ¼ inch inside the seam lines. This means that there are a lot of thread ends to be tied and buried, but the quilting itself is so fast that the

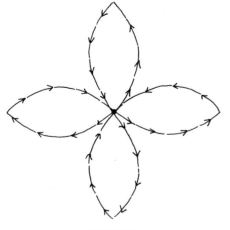

FIGURE 3
Begin stitching at the dot in the middle and follow the arrows.

20

overall time needed to finish a quilt this way is still a great deal less than if the work were to be done by hand. It is really a pleasant job to stitch for a while, then sit down and relax while tying off the ends.

To finish the machine-stitched thread ends, pull them to the wrong side of the quilt, tie them, then thread the ends into a needle to bury them in the batting, cutting them off close to the surface. Some quilters who use the machine begin and end their stitching with several very small stitches, then simply cut off the ends close to the fabric. This method is all right, but certainly not as neat as burying the tied ends.

If you study your quilt before beginning to quilt by machine, it will be apparent that there are ways to stitch to minimize the number of threads to tie off. Begin working in the center of the quilt, stitching long lines first if possible. On a quilt like Patched Hearts (page 107), stitch the long lines of the sashing in both directions first, to stabilize the layers, then quilt inside the blocks. If the quilt has been basted well, there will be no tucks on the back.

Some of the blocks are ornamented with stitching in a pattern designed to keep the number of ends to a minimum. When stitching a pattern like that in Figure 3, begin stitching in the middle at the dot and follow the arrows to complete the design, leaving only two beginning and two ending threads with which to deal.

Machine-quilt with a stitch length of about 4 mm or 4 to 6 stitches to the inch, using the accessory quilting presser foot or engaging the dual-feed if your machine is equipped with it. This will ensure that both the top and bottom layers of the quilt are fed through the machine at the same rate. Guide the quilt as the machine stitches, but let the feed dogs do the actual work of moving the layers under the needle to ensure even stitches. Do not stitch over the pins. Remove them as the stitching comes close to them. Change the machine needle after four or five hours of stitching, even if the needle seems fine. A new needle is *not* a luxury.

Finishing

When all the quilting has been completed, trim the layers to the measurements noted in the instructions. Usually the batting starts out an inch wider than the top and backing, because there may be a little shifting and the batting seems to be the layer that takes it up. When the batting is low-loft, sometimes the finished edge of the quilt is fluffier if the batting is cut the same as the other two layers and turned in when the raw edges are whipstitched together. Other times, when that would be too bulky, the batting should be cut a seam's width shorter than the top and back. Look to the individual quilt's instructions for advice about this.

There are a number of ways to finish the outside edges of a quilt. Several have been utilized in the projects in this book, and the basic instructions for those follow.

QUILT EDGE FINISHES

Bias binding and corded piping are two elegant, tailored finishes often found on beautiful quilts. Both are easily applied and not only hold the layers together and finish the edges, but also add their own particular beauty and a dash of color, if wanted, to the edges of a quilt. They are generally interchangeable, but the binding usually finishes a bit wider than the piping, sometimes dictating the choice.

Cutting and Preparing Bias Strips

Both bias binding and the fabric covering for corded piping are usually cut on the true bias of the fabric. This means that the first cut is made diagonally from corner to corner on a square of fabric as shown on the drawing (Figure 1). The subsequent cuts are made the width specified in the instructions and following the line of the first cut.

(Some quiltmakers cut the strips for both piping and binding on the straight grain of the fabric and finish their quilts with perfect results. However, the bias cut allows a perfect finish with much less effort. To use bias or not is a decision for the quilter to make. In this book it is assumed that bias will be used, and materials and cutting directions are specified for that.)

The bias strips may be joined into seams as often as necessary to make one long strip to enclose the edges of a quilt. If these seams are made as the directions indicate, they will be almost invisible.

Determine the total number of inches of bias strips needed to finish a quilt by adding the sum of the sides and adding about 12 inches for corners and the end seam. Then add ½ inch for each seam when the strips need to be pieced together, to obtain the needed length. Most quilters routinely make a strip longer than the estimated length just as insurance against having to add a piece at the end.

When the strips are cut on the true bias, the ends are also on the slant. To join two pieces in a seam, hold them right sides together as in the drawing (Figure 2) and make a ¼-inch seam. Stitch all the pieces together to make one long strip. Trim the seams to ⅛ inch and press them open. The strip is now ready to be attached to the quilt or made into piping.

Corded Piping

With the wrong side of the bias strip facing up, lay the cord at the center of the strip parallel to the edges as shown in Figure 3.

Fold the bias in half, enclosing the cord as shown in Figure 4. Using a cording presser foot and holding the cord so it stays along the fold, stitch as close to the cord as possible for the length of the strip. Use a straight stitch with a utility length—about 10 stitches to the inch on older machines, about 2 mm on newer machines.

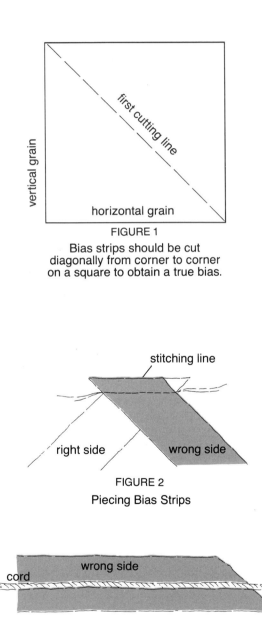

FIGURE 1

Bias strips should be cut
diagonally from corner to corner
on a square to obtain a true bias.

FIGURE 2

Piecing Bias Strips

FIGURE 3

Trim the raw edges of the fabric to a straight line, leaving a ¼-inch seam allowance.

The cording is now ready to be inserted into the outer seam of the quilt. The best practice is to stitch the cording to the finished quilt top before the layers are assembled. Use the stitching line on the cording as a guide and stitch as close to it as possible. Then after the quilting is complete, it remains only to trim the edges of the layers, turn the raw edges to the inside, and whipstitch the backing to the top along the stitching line of the cording.

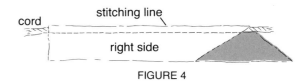

FIGURE 4

Bias Binding

Cut and seam the bias binding as instructed on page 22. After all quilting is complete, trim the three layers of the quilt to an even ½-inch seam allowance. Beginning at the center of the bottom of the quilt and with right sides together, stitch the binding to the quilt in a ½-inch seam, allowing enough extra at the corners to make a neat miter.

Trim the edges if the finished binding is to be less than ½ inch, or if there are any uneven places.

Press the seam flat and turn the binding to the back. Turn the raw edge to the inside and stitch by hand to finish.

SPECIAL TOUCHES FOR YOUR QUILT

Antiquing Fabric

As our fondness for re-creating old quilts grows, it becomes increasingly easy to find reproductions of old patterns and new fabrics that are copies of antiques, which add greatly to the authenticity of our products. Sometimes, though, no matter how perfect the fabrics and technique, the finished quilt still looks new, especially if it is used in a setting with old pieces. Age adds a special kind of softness—yes, and also some yellowing and spotting we could do without.

While it is really almost impossible to duplicate what the years add to a piece, it is sometimes possible to create the aura of antiquity by treating fabrics with a dye solution made from coffee or tea. If you have ever tried to remove a tea or coffee stain from a good tablecloth, you know that tea and coffee are fairly permanent dyes and certainly endure enough to last through many washings. Although only one of the quilts in this book has been "antiqued" by the method that follows, antiquing fabric is fun and does dramatically add "age" to new products. Most of the other quilts could be treated this way to make them fit into a country or period setting.

You should be aware, however, that this is not an exact science and what follows does not contain any formulas to be followed to the letter. Don't run to the kitchen with your new quilt yet!

Either coffee or tea may be used for the dye solution. They produce different shades of brown. Tea seems to give a more red or orange cast, while coffee gives a deep rich brown. Both are lovely. The only way to decide which to use is to make test samples on the fabric of the quilt.

Note that this color process works only on natural fibers—cotton, linen, and silk. You will find that each takes the dye differently.

The Dyeing Process

Wash the fabric thoroughly to remove the sizing, and rinse it well. Roll it in a towel to remove the excess dripping water, but do not dry it. The dye will take more evenly if the fabric is wet when immersed into it.

Brew the tea or coffee to make a fairly strong solution. Make enough to partially fill a pot large enough to allow the fabric to be submerged completely. Bring the brew to a boil in the pot. Add about ½ cup white vinegar per quart of coffee or tea.

If you are dyeing a piece of fabric large enough for the back of a quilt, or if you are "antiquing" the fabrics for patchwork prior to cutting them, immerse the wet fabric in the brew and boil it about ten minutes, lifting it out of the dye several times to check the depth of coloration. The fabric will be a little lighter when dry. Rinse well. Roll in a towel, press out excess water, then iron dry.

To "antique" a sewn piece of patchwork, wet the piece thoroughly. Roll it in a towel to remove the excess water. Place the wet piece on an old towel, then paint on the dye with a camel hair brush. Add the color selectively where you think an old quilt would have aged to brown shades. For a piece like the little Antique Hearts on page 71, after the quilt top was stenciled and the colored borders added, it was wet and coffee was painted along all the seam lines. The solution was applied more heavily directly on the seam lines and allowed to bleed into the adjacent fabric. The quilt backing and the fabric for the binding were dipped in coffee and ironed before the quilt was assembled.

Usually, painting on dye adds more age than does the immersion method because the final effect is more patchy. If possible, paint on the coffee or tea before your quilt has been finished, to avoid the dye solution seeping into the batting. If it does and you have used a coffee dye, there will be a slight odor of coffee for a short time. This is usually not a big problem, but one you should be aware might happen.

Shadow Embroidery

The instructions that follow are for the easy basic method of doing shadow embroidery from the right side, using the double-back or herringbone stitch illustrated below. The fabric should be sheer to allow the color, which is on the the wrong side, to show through. Hence the name shadow embroidery.

Trace the embroidery design onto the right side of the fabric, using a #2 pencil or a washout marker.

Work the stitches with a single strand of embroidery floss and either a #7 crewel or a #26 tapestry needle. The large needle makes it easy to see to reenter the same holes while stitching.

Work with the fabric stretched lightly in an embroidery hoop, and use the sewing motion shown in the drawings. Work from right to left.

On the stitch drawings, the needle is shown by long dashes where it is behind the fabric. The thread under the fabric is shown by a series of shorter dashes. Notice that the needle always uses the same hole as the previous stitch. The needle always comes to the surface from the back in a place where there is no thread. The downward stitch is into a hole already occupied by a thread. This prevents splitting the thread when the stitch comes to the surface.

To practice the stitch, draw a pair of parallel lines about ¼ inch apart on a small piece of sheer fabric and place it in an embroidery hoop. Although the work should be done without knots, tie a knot for the practice piece and learn the stitch first. Thereafter, begin and end without knots, placing the tying stitches under the backstitches that appear on the right side.

Step 1: Bring the needle to the surface at A and make a backstitch to B. Bring the needle to the surface again at C, which is on the lower line directly below A. Pull the thread through.

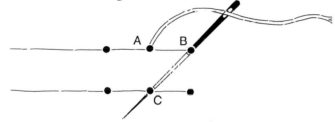

Step 2: With the thread in position as shown, make a backstitch to D and bring the needle to the surface at E, on the top line. Pull the thread through.

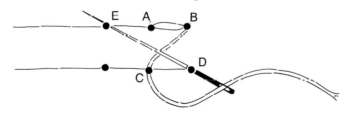

Step 3: Make a stitch back to A (this is stitch F), going into exactly the same hole as A. Bring the needle up again on the lower line at G.

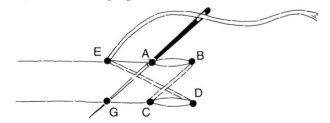

Step 4: Backstitch to C to make stitch H. Come up on I on the upper line. Follow this sequence, keeping the stitches even and always going down into exactly the same hole used by the previous stitch. Turn the hoop over and notice the way the threads cross each other. Notice also that the smaller the stitches, the more apparent the color.

Stenciling Supplies
Stencil film
Brushes
Fabric paint or stencil crayons
Crafts knife
Cutting board
Tracing paper
Ruler
Felt-tip pen
Paper towels
Saucer or other paint container
Brush cleaner

Stenciling on Fabric

Most fabrics traditionally used for quilting can be successfully stenciled. Check the label of the paint to be certain it is compatible with the fiber content of your fabric, and that it will be washable after correct setting of the color.

Fabric to be decorated with a stencil pattern should be washed to remove the sizing. Otherwise, the paint will sit on top of the sizing and wash off when the sizing is removed by the first washing.

The stenciled quilts in this book have been colored with either fabric paint or stencil crayons. Both are easy to use and produce dependable results.

The fabric paints are usually latex or acrylic and have been formulated to a good consistency for dry-brush stenciling. They dry quickly and can be cleaned up with water. Craft stores stock a wide range of colors and several different brands.

The stencil crayon is a unique product combining linseed oil and pigment in a compressed wax base. It is the most mistake-proof paint available. Not only is it easy to use, it is fun! The color is applied to the stencil film, then brushed onto the surface to be colored. It will dry overnight and leaves the fabric soft.

The stencil brush is stubby, with blunt-cut bristles. It is good to have a separate brush for each color to be used. After use, clean up with brush cleaner, water, or turpentine as the paint manufacturer suggests.

Stencil film is inexpensive and found in most craft or art supply stores. Cut it on a cutting board with a craft knife.

Stenciling a Quilt

The Materials list with your project will detail the paints and amount of film needed for the quilt. Under Finding the Materials, there are tips about finding the colors used in the quilt shown in the photograph.

Follow the instructions for stenciling your quilt for guidance in tracing and cutting the stencils. In some of the designs, two separate stencils must be cut for one color, even though they will be painted with the same paint.

When you get ready to stencil a project, collect the materials and tools you will need and assemble them on a desk or table. Protect the tabletop with a cutting board while you are cutting the stencils. Place a clean white paper under the fabric to absorb any excess paint that accumulates. These pieces are so small that you can hold them taut enough to paint with your hand or several pieces of tape.

If you are using fabric paint or dye, use the dry-brush method. Place a small amount of paint in a shallow container. Holding the brush upright, dip just the tips into the paint. Work the brush in a circular motion on a paper towel or other scrap paper until the paint is almost gone. Notice that in the beginning little swirled lines of paint appear. When they are gone and only a soft, even layer of color remains, the brush is ready to begin on your fabric.

Always work the brush in a circular motion away from the cut edge (so the paint does not get underneath the stencil). To achieve shading, work more heavily in one area. Follow manufacturer's instructions to set the color.

To color a design with a stencil crayon, draw some color onto the stencil film along the edges of the opening of the area to be painted. Use the brush and a circular motion to work the paint onto the fabric. You can shade or paint solid areas of color. The paint usually dries overnight and does not need special treatment to set the color.

It is a good idea to practice painting a motif on paper or scrap fabric to check the stencil, the colors of the paints, and your shading. The design for Bluebirds for Baby, shown on page 138, has been stenciled with crayons and printed in color as a guide for painting with that medium. Notice the way the use of two stencils for the blue allows the shading around the birds' wings and breasts. This shading is also noticeable in the ribbons. Little touches with a fabric pen make the eyes bright and smiling.

If you have never tried stenciling on fabric, you will enjoy one of these little projects. If you have ever appliquéd a quilt, you will see why stenciling has been such a stand-by for centuries.

BASIC QUILTING TERMS

Appliqué. A decorative technique usually used to attach a fabric decoration to another fabric.

Backing. The fabric used for the back or undecorated side of a quilt.

Basting. Long temporary stitches used to hold pieces together during handling or final construction.

Batting. The fluffy inner layer of a quilt; it adds warmth and loft.

Bearding. The migration of batting fibers through the outside fabric of a quilt.

Bias. Fabric cut at a 45-degree angle to the selvages to maximize stretch and drape.

Binding. A narrow strip of fabric—usually bias—used to finish the edges of a quilt.

Block. A term used to describe one unit of a quilt design.

Fat quarter. A popular way to cut a quarter yard of fabric so it can be used to its best advantage. A half yard is cut across the full width of the fabric. This is then cut in half vertically to make two pieces 18 × 22 inches—two fat quarters.

Field. The pieced or ornamented quilt top minus the borders.

Grain. The horizontal and vertical threads of fabric.

Lattice block. The square that is used to connect lattice strips when two colors are used.

Lattice strip. Strips of fabric used to join the blocks of a quilt top.

Loft. The degree of thickness of batting.

Miter. A method of joining corners at 45-degree angles, as for a picture frame.

Piecing. Stitching together small pieces of fabric to make a patchwork design.

Quilting. The stitching that holds together the three layers of a quilt, at the same time adding decoration and texture.

Sashing. Another term for lattice strips.

Set. The way in which the decorative blocks of a quilt are assembled.

Shadow embroidery. An embroidery technique that places the bulk of the colored thread on the wrong side of a sheer fabric.

Shadow quilting. A quilting method that places colored fabric under a sheer fabric.

Stitch in the ditch. The placement of a row of stitching in the groove of a seam line.

Template. A piece of plastic, cardboard, or paper used as a guide for tracing quilting designs or for cutting out patchwork pieces.

Whipstitch. A small, invisible hand-sewing stitch used to finish the edges of a quilt.

THE
QUILT COLLECTION

SIMPLICITY

A CUDDLY FAVORITE FOR THE CRIB
Finished size: 40½″ × 50½″

CLASSIC ELEGANCE RESULTING FROM A combination of soft colors and simple block quilting distinguishes this favorite quilt. It is especially refreshing as a decorative accessory now, when every piece of nursery linen and infant clothing seems to be embellished with a cartoon character or wild jungle animal. This easy-to-make crib cover will be a most appreciated gift.

If you have never made a quilt, this is the one with which to start. It will acquaint you with the basic quilting terms, give you a good chance to do some pretty stitching by hand or machine, and teach you to make and attach corded piping. The project will be finished quickly, soon ready to snuggle some lucky baby.

Materials

Pink batiste, poly cotton blend, 44″ wide—1½ yards

Pale blue batiste, poly-cotton blend, 44″ wide—1½ yards

White batiste, poly-cotton blend, 44″ wide—½ yard

Extra-loft polyester quilt batting—crib size

Machine quilting thread to match both pink and blue fabrics

White sewing thread

Cotton cording—6 yards

Finding the Materials

The fabric chosen for the photographed quilt is a tightly woven poly-cotton batiste printed with tiny white flowers. All three colors are of the same pattern. Alternate colors will make a very different quilt. The possibilities are endless.

You can save making the corded piping if you use purchased piping. Buy 6 yards of white piping instead of the ½ yard white batiste and the 6 yards cotton cording in the Materials list.

The extra-loft batting is especially fluffy and warm when quilted like this. If you opt to hand-quilt, change the batting to a traditional or low loft to allow for smaller stitches. The extra loft that was used in the finished quilt makes a fluffy quilt that, when machine-stitched, can be finished in a matter of hours.

Before you begin working, check the Basic Sewing Supplies list on page 11 and the Basic Quilting Supplies list on page 12 to make sure you have everything you will need on hand.

Cutting Guide

From the white batiste cut enough
1¼-inch-wide bias strips to
piece into a 6-yard length.
The pink and blue batistes are
already cut to the right length.
Check to make certain they
are straight.

LAYOUT DRAWING

Assembly

Following the instructions on page 22, make 6 yards of white corded piping.

With the right side up, spread the pink batiste flat and draw a 42 × 54-inch rectangle on it. Following the Layout Drawing, draw the quilting grid. A blue washout pen is a good marker for this step.

With the raw edges matching, stitch the white piping to the edge of the pink batiste, allowing a ½-inch seam line. It is best to begin and end the piping at the center of one of the short sides of the quilt, assuming that side will be the bottom.

Place the blue batiste on a flat surface with the wrong side facing up. Spread the batting smoothly on top. Finish with the pink, right side up. Pin securely. Baste, placing the rows of stitches about 2 inches apart. Baste in both directions so the layers won't slip during the quilting.

Use the pink thread on the top of the machine, the blue on the bobbin. Stitch with the pink side facing up. Set the machine for a straight stitch about 4 mm long or 5 stitches to the inch. Use a quilting or dual-feed presser foot to keep the layers feeding at the same rate. Stitch on all the drawn lines.

Pull all the thread ends to one side of the quilt, tie them, then thread them into a needle and bury them in the quilt batting. Cut the ends off short.

Trim the batting so it is ½ inch shorter than the pink-and-blue batiste on all sides. Turn the raw edges of the pink and blue fabric to the inside and whipstitch the edge closed with invisible stitches.

CELEBRATION

AN EXUBERANT LITTLE NINE-PATCH
Finished size: 33″ × 46″

Although it is a basic nine-patch design, when the exuberant colors of this quilt were first spread on the floor to arrange the patches, it was named Celebration. Its roots in the old design and its use of cotton calicos and batting celebrate the traditions of quilting, but it is so much fun to plan and stitch that the whole project is a celebration!

The cotton batting and the machine quilting with nylon thread make a quilt with an interesting texture. This might be the quilt you want to tea-dye to make it look antique.

Although the pictured quilt has been machine-quilted, there are many little squares to stitch and thus many thread ends to tie and bury. Even so, the machine quilting is not a tremendous job and is certainly finished much more quickly than quilting by hand.

Finding the Materials

The little Nine-Patch squares that make the field of the quilt were made from a packet of 2-inch die-cut squares bought at a quilt shop. They were all cotton, two each of a wide assortment of tiny prints—just the kind of surprise a quilter loves even when she has no plans for its use!

The collection of prints included light blue, medium blue, navy, yellow, medium green, rose, red, dark red, brown, tan, and plum. All are bright hues and each one is a small floral print. If this kind of assortment is not available, buy an assortment of small prints or use remnants already on hand. You need only two 2 × 2-inch squares of each print. Allowing for shrinkage, a fat quarter can be cut into about eighty squares. Cut a few squares of the two border prints and the backing print to tie your assortment together.

Before you begin working, check the Basic Sewing Supplies list on page 11 and the Basic Quilting Supplies list on page 12 to make sure you have everything you will need on hand.

Materials

White muslin, 100% cotton,
    42″ wide—1 yard
Assorted scrap fabrics or
    ¼-yard pieces of bright prints,
    100% cotton
Navy calico print, 100% cotton,
    42″ wide—1½ yards
Red geometric print, 100% cotton,
    42″ wide—1½ yards
Yellow calico print, 100% cotton,
    42″ wide—1½ yards
Cotton batting—crib size
Transparent nylon quilting thread

36

```
┌──────────────────────────────────────┐
│                                      │
│                                      │
│                                      │
│                                      │
│                                      │
│                                      │
│                                      │
│             TEMPLATE 2               │
│                                      │
│                                      │
│                                      │
│                                      │
│                                      │
│                                      │
│                                      │
└──────────────────────────────────────┘
```

Cutting Guide

From the white muslin cut:
 96 squares 2 × 2 inches
 (Template 1)
 35 squares 5 × 5 inches
 (Template 2)
From the red print cut:
 2 strips 2 × 47 inches
 2 strips 2 × 36 inches
From the navy calico cut:
 2 strips 5 × 47 inches
 2 strips 5 × 36 inches
 Enough 1½-inch bias strips to
 total 165 inches
From the yellow calico cut:
 The quilt backing, 36 × 49
 inches
From the assorted scrap fabrics cut:
 120 calico squares 2 × 2 inches
 assorted as follows: light blue,
 9; medium blue, 22; navy, 10;
 yellow, 14; medium green, 21;
 rose, 4; red, 16; dark red, 8;
 brown, 8; tan, 3; plum, 5.

To Assemble One Nine-Patch Block

Figure 1 illustrates one complete Nine-Patch square, one of the most basic quilt designs. Although the drawing is shown in two colors, the blocks can also be constructed with three colors for a little more variety. This works best if the center square is one color and the four corners another color. To use the scrap look effectively, the blocks of Celebration incorporate still another variation: The four corners are all the same color, but in most cases those four squares are cut from two different prints.

```
┌──────────────────────┐
│                      │
│                      │
│                      │
│     TEMPLATE 1       │
│                      │
│                      │
│                      │
└──────────────────────┘
```

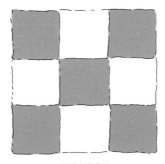

One Complete Nine-Patch Block

FIGURE 1

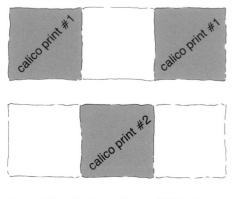

FIGURE 2

To make one block, choose one square for the center, four of another color for the corners, and four white squares. Lay the squares out in three rows as in Figure 2. Use calico print #1 for the colored squares of Row 1, the single calico print #2 for the center of Row 2, the two calico print #3 squares in Row 3. Prints #1 and #3 are the same color but a different print.

Allowing a ¼-inch seam allowance, stitch the three squares of each row into a strip as shown by Figure 2. Trim the seams to ⅛ inch and press the seams toward the color. Join the three rows, matching the seam lines carefully. Trim the seams and press.

Assembling the Quilt Top

Spread out the collection of colored 2-inch squares and decide how they will be combined into blocks.

Following the directions above, combine the colored squares with the white ones and construct twenty-four Nine-Patch blocks. Press all seams as they are stitched, then press the blocks.

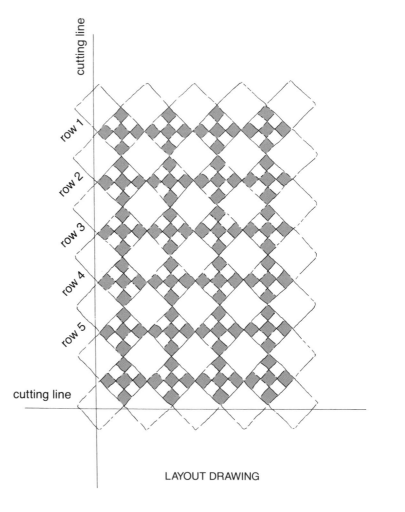

LAYOUT DRAWING

TEMPLATE 3

Lay out the twenty-four blocks, placing them on point—rotated so that a point, rather than the flat side of a block, is at both bottom and top. Arrange in the most pleasing color distribution. Follow the Layout Drawing and make six rows of four blocks each.

Arrange the seven rows of 5-inch white squares, alternating them with the pieced blocks as shown in the Layout Drawing.

Beginning with Row 2, stitch the pieced blocks to the white squares in the diagonal rows. After stitching and pressing each row, put it back in position. Join the diagonal rows to complete the pieced field.

Lay a straightedge along the sides as shown in the Layout Drawing, and cut away the surplus white to make an even edge. Notice that the cutting line is a seam allowance beyond (¼ inch) the points of the blocks.

Borders

Stitch the 36-inch red border strips to the 36-inch navy strips. Repeat for the 47-inch lengths of both. Trim the seams and press.

Pin the red border edges to the trimmed edges of the pieced top, allowing the extra length to extend equally at both ends of the border pieces. Stitch,

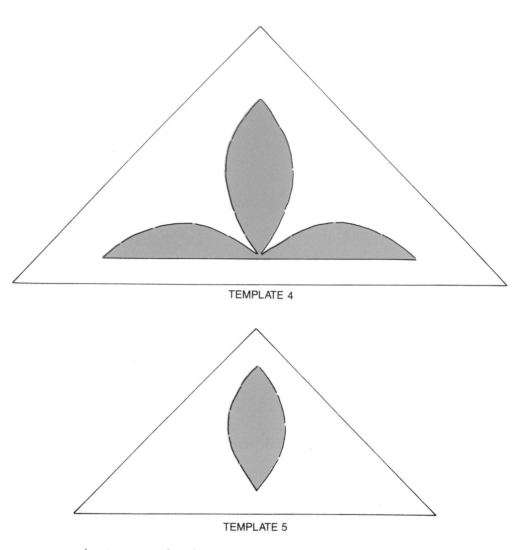

TEMPLATE 4

TEMPLATE 5

beginning and ending ¼ inch from each end. Fold the extensions to form a miter and stitch all four corners. If there is a little extra length in the borders, trim it off. Trim the seams and press.

Cut a template for each of the three quilting patterns—Templates 3, 4, and 5. Cut the template to match the square or triangle, then cut out the blue portion of the design. Place the template on the white patch to be marked, matching the edges of the template to the edges of the patch to center the quilting design. Trace the patterns on all the white portions of the quilt top. Template 3 fits the full squares, Template 4 is for the triangles at the edges, and Template 5 finishes the little corner triangles.

Final Assembly and Quilting

Spread the yellow calico backing piece flat with the wrong side up. Place the batting on top and follow with the quilt top right side up. If there is a lot of excess batting, trim it, but leave an inch extra on all sides.

Pin the layers together securely. For machine quilting—which is easiest with the cotton batting—pin with inch-long nickel-plated safety pins placed 2 inches apart, or hand-baste, placing rows 2 inches apart both horizontally and vertically.

Machine-quilt with transparent nylon thread, following the Quilting Guide drawing. Quilt on every line shown on the drawing except the lines showing the bias binding. Some of these lines represent "in the ditch" stitching, the balance are inside the squares. (If you have never tried machine quilting, refer to Machine Quilting on page 20 for directions.)

When all the quilting has been completed, trim the edges of the batting and backing if needed. Following the instructions on page 23, finish the edges with navy bias binding.

QUILTING GUIDE

ELEGANCE

A ONE-PIECE COUNTERPANE
Finished size: 41″ × 53″

THE ONE-PIECE COUNTERPANE HAS AL-
ways been a favorite of quilters who love the tranquility of the quilting stitch. The linsey-
woolsey spreads from Colonial days often incorporated very complicated designs that must
have taken days to lay out and mark for quilting. Since they were so time-consuming, most
were kept for "good," and thus many have survived to become museum pieces for us to enjoy.

The beauty of this style of quilt is that it depends solely on the hand quilting for its design
and texture. While this little version is much simplified, it is still a very traditional design,
with plenty of hand stitching to bring to life the delicate Prince William feathers and scrolls
against the elegant chevron background.

Materials

White-on-white print, 100%
   cotton, 42″ wide—3½ yards
Traditional batting—crib size
Cotton cording—5½ yards
#50 white cotton mercerized
   thread for quilting and
   construction
Tracing paper—1 piece 23″ × 30″
   and 4 sheets 12″ × 12″
Black pen with medium point
Washout pen or 4H pencil
Masking tape—½″ wide

Finding the Materials

The white-on-white print adds a subtle contemporary touch to this very
traditional quilt. If this fabric is not available, other choices that would be
beautiful are cotton sateen, Sea Island cotton, or a fine white muslin. To retain
the elegance but add another interest, consider using some color—make
both sides a wonderful pastel or keep one side white while using a color for
the backing.

Since there is so much hand quilting and small stitches are prettiest on these
rounded shapes, it is best not to substitute a higher-loft batting.

Before you begin working, check the Basic Sewing Supplies list on page 11
and the Basic Quilting Supplies list on page 12 to make sure you have
everything you will need on hand.

Cutting Guide

From the white-on-white cotton
  cut:
The quilt top, 42 × 54 inches
The quilt back, 42 × 54 inches
White bias strips 1½ inches wide,
  to total 192 inches

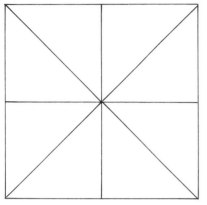

FIGURE 1

Laying Out the Pattern

The best way to transfer a design like this to the fabric is to make a complete tracing of one-fourth of the quilt, assembling all the various designs on paper, and then trace the entire design onto the fabric. Follow the step-by-step instructions to make a drawing, then go over it with a pen that makes a mark black enough to trace through the fabric.

The Feather Medallion

On a 12 × 12-inch piece of tracing paper draw an 11-inch square. Draw the four lines dividing the square into eight triangles, as shown in Figure 1.

Place the tracing paper over the drawing of the medallion feather—Figure 2—matching the guidelines on the feather to those on the tracing paper. Trace one feather. Notice on the drawing of the quilt that all the feathers in the center medallion turn in the same direction. To place the next one, rotate the tracing paper to line up the next pair of guidelines and trace the feather again. Continue around the "spokes" of the medallion until eight feathers have been traced. Set this drawing aside for the time being.

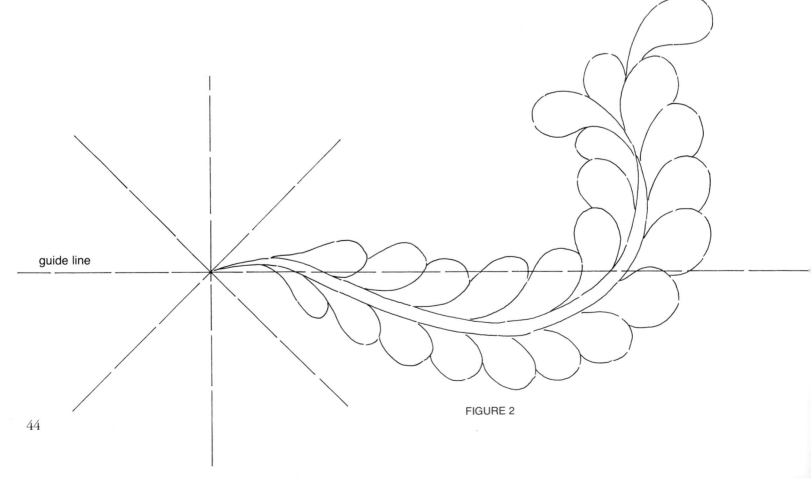

guide line

FIGURE 2

44

45

The Basic Layout

Figure 3 represents one-quarter of the quilt. The top and right-side lines are the folds of the fabric, the left line is the selvage, and the bottom line is the cut edge.

On the large sheet of tracing paper, copy the drawing. Make the drawing as accurate as possible.

Begin by drawing a rectangle 21 × 27 inches. Measure in 1½ inches from the sides of the rectangle and draw Line 1. Next draw Line 2 exactly ½ inch inside Line 1.

Line 3 is 7 inches inside Line 2. Line 4 is ½ inch from Line 3.

Line 5 is 2 inches from Line 4. Line 6 is ½ inch from Line 5.

Draw the diagonal line through the corners, extending it to the edge of the rectangle as shown on the drawing.

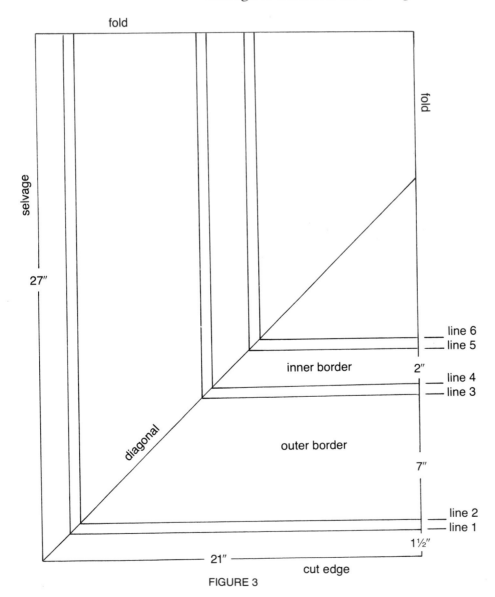

FIGURE 3

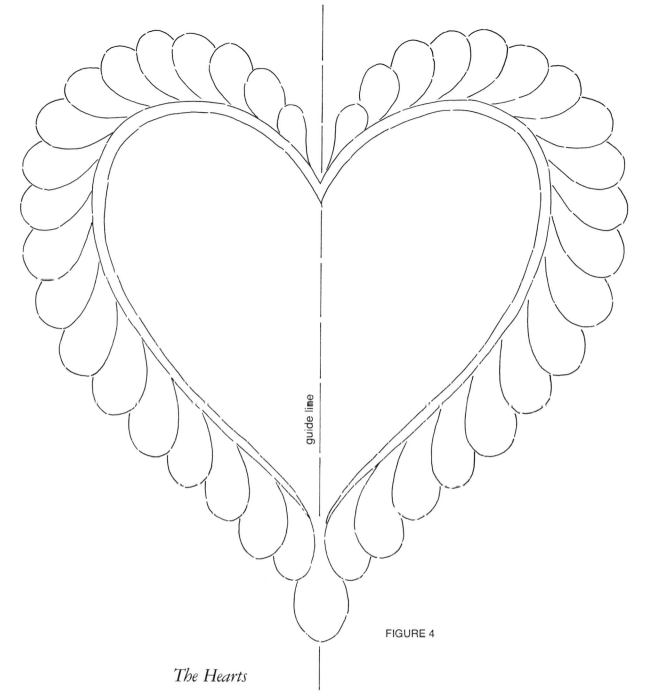

guide line

FIGURE 4

The Hearts

Trace the heart motif (Figure 4) onto a piece of tracing paper. Use the Layout Drawing (page 50) as a reference for placing the various elements on your large drawing.

Match the guideline through the heart with the diagonal line to place a heart inside Line 6. Place the heart on the diagonal with the tip of the guideline that extends from the base of the heart at the point at which the lines intersect at the corner. Trace two half hearts, placing them at the fold lines, between Lines 2 and 3, again using the center line to help with placement.

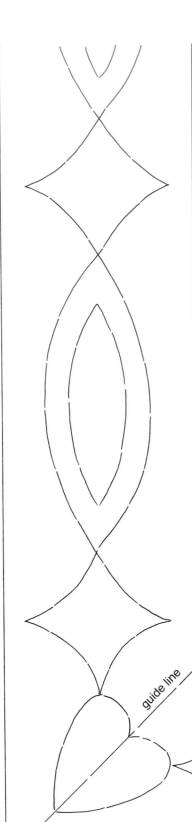

Inner Border

Next trace the inner border (Figure 5) and copy it on the large drawing. Begin tracing at the corner, matching the diagonal line and following the Layout Drawing for the number of repeats to reach the fold lines. Notice that on the long side, the diamond repeats three times.

Outside Border

Trace the large feather scroll (Figure 6). In addition to this tracing, you also need a reverse drawing of this feather. To make this, turn the traced paper over and trace it again on the wrong side.

Use the diagonal to line up the scroll at the corner. Trace one side, then use the reversed drawing to trace the other half of the corner.

On the bottom edge of the piece, still following the Layout Drawing, place the reverse side of the feather scroll in the space between the heart and the corner scroll, using just the portion of the scroll needed to fill the space. Keep the spacing along the edges the same as that of the first scroll.

On the long side of the rectangle, repeat the second scroll and add a third one turned as shown in the Layout Drawing. Use the Layout Drawing as a guide for placement of these scrolls. It shows in detail the way they are "tucked" under the other scrolls.

Do not trace the center medallion on the large drawing. It is shown on the Layout Drawing only as a reference.

guide line

FIGURE 5

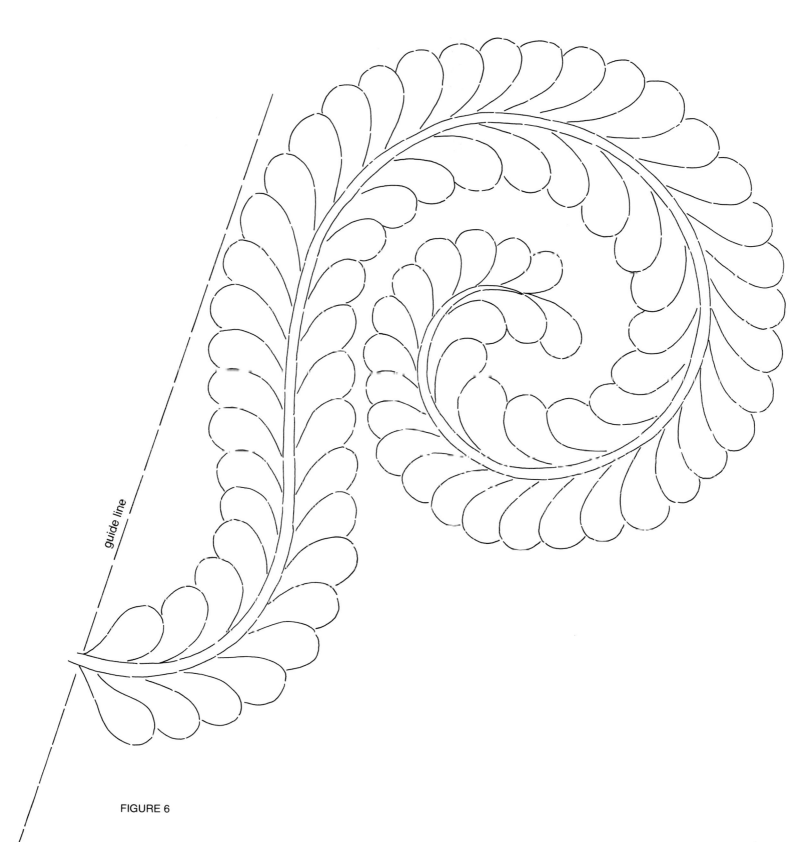

guide line

FIGURE 6

49

50

LAYOUT DRAWING

Marking the Quilt Top

Lay the ironed fabric on a large flat surface. Make certain it is straight. Divide it into four quarters. If your fabric is 42 inches wide, each quarter will measure 21×27 inches. Draw the lines dividing the fabric into quarters.

Pin or tape the drawing under the quilt top, matching the lines dividing the fabric with the outlines of the rectangle on the paper. Trace the entire drawing, including the diagonal.

Repeat the tracing on all four sections.

Matching the guidelines of the center medallion drawing to the lines at the center of the quilt top, trace the medallion.

Assembly and Quilting

Layer the quilt backing, the batting, and the top, carefully matching the selvage edges. Pin the layers together and then baste them firmly, in both horizontal and vertical rows about 2 inches apart.

Beginning at the center, quilt the medallion, then work outward, stitching the hearts and the borders. Quilt on all lines except the horizontal and vertical lines dividing the quilt into quarters.

Chevron Background

Use the drawing of the quilt (page 45) as a guide for the chevron background in the center field. Begin stitching at the inner border at the diagonal on one side. Stitch through the center of the heart, then to the center line. At the center line, turn and follow the diagonal line of the adjoining quarter to the inner border on that side. This inverted "V" establishes the start of the lines for the chevron pattern.

For all subsequent lines, lay a piece of masking tape along the just stitched line, then quilt along the other side of the tape. Carry the chevron pattern through to cover the entire center field. When rows intersect the center medallion, end the stitching there.

When rows intersect the hearts, carry the pattern through the hearts to the inner border on the other side.

Complete all the quilting, including the parallel lines in Figure 3.

Trim the edges if they are not perfectly even. Use the bias strips to make corded piping, following the instructions on page 22. Holding the batting and the backing out of the way, stitch the piping to the quilt top.

Turn the raw edges to the inside, and fasten the seam with invisible stitches.

SWEET DREAMS

A SHADOW-EMBROIDERED COMFORTER
Finished size: 40″ × 60″

This FLUFFY, EASY-CARE COMFORTER will be a favorite in the nursery. The white squares are embellished with six folk art bird motifs worked in pastel pink, blue, yellow, and green shadow embroidery. Further, each square is outlined with Victorian Crazy Quilt embroidery that adds more color at the seams. A very full double ruffle finishes the edges.

The matching decorative pillows are pretty in the crib during the day. They can also be used on the rocking chair or in the carriage. They can be made up as squares as shown, or two motifs can be combined to make an oblong pillow.

Finding the Materials

This cloud-soft quilt takes advantage of the best qualities of the blended fabrics. Choose fabric that is woven tightly so the batting won't migrate through. You might also want to consider that the basic blue of the quilt can be changed to pink, yellow, or green without changing the embroidery colors. This comforter is particularly pretty in yellow.

Choose a sheer batiste for the embroidered squares. Take the batiste with you to choose the embroidery floss colors. As the bulk of the thread will be on the wrong side of the embroidery, place the skeins *under* one layer of batiste to see if the color will be strong enough to be effective.

The lining fabric can be the same batiste as that used for the embroidered squares, or you can use a less expensive white fabric. The lining serves two purposes: It protects the long stitches on the back, and it provides a denser back than the batting would, allowing the embroidery more prominence.

This comforter is tied at the corners of the squares and has no quilting at all. Therefore it is prettiest with the extra thickness of a high-loft batting.

Before you begin working, check the Basic Sewing Supplies list on page 11 and the Basic Quilting Supplies list on page 12 to make sure you have everything you will need on hand. Check page 24 for basic shadow embroidery instructions and a diagram of the stitch used.

Materials

Pale blue broadcloth, poly-cotton blend, 42″ wide—5¾ yards
White batiste, poly-cotton blend, 42″ wide—1¼ yards
White lining fabric, 42″ wide—1¼ yards
Extra-loft quilt batting—crib size
Six-strand cotton embroidery floss—5 skeins pink, 5 skeins blue, 5 skeins yellow, and 3 skeins green
Blue and white machine sewing thread
Size 7 crewel needle
(Materials for the matching pillows are listed on page 61.)

Cutting Guide

From the blue broadcloth cut:

The comforter back,
42 × 62 inches

2 strips 4 × 62 inches

2 pieces 4 × 37 inches

5 pieces 3 × 37 inches

18 lattice pieces 3 × 8 inches

Enough 7-inch-wide strips to piece together a 14-yard ruffle

From the white lining fabric cut:

24 squares, 8 × 8 inches

Leave the 1¼-yard piece of white batiste intact.

The Shadow Embroidery

It is easiest to work the shadow embroidery in a hoop if there is a little extra fabric around the 8-inch squares. Therefore it is best to leave the squares connected. Also, if your fabric happens to be 45 inches wide, do not cut the extra away until the finished embroidery is cut apart.

Divide the 45 inches of batiste into twenty-four squares measuring 8 × 8 inches. The squares can touch on all four sides. Leave the little bit of extra fabric at the edges. You can mark the divisions by pulled threads or by carefully drawing them.

Trace the six embroidery motifs. Transfer each motif to four different batiste squares. Separate the six strands of embroidery floss and, following the colors shown in embroidery motifs, work all the shadow embroidery with two strands in the size 7 crewel needle to give the quilt a bit more color than the traditional single strand would impart. (Refer to Shadow Embroidery on page 24 for help with the embroidery.)

Some of the stitches in these designs are rather long, but since the embroidery will be lined, that will present no problems.

Embroider all twenty-four squares. Wash if necessary to remove markings. Iron dry on a padded surface, without touching the right side of the embroidery with the iron. Cut the squares apart.

Assembling the Quilt Top

Pin or baste one lining piece to the back of each embroidered square.

Lay the squares on a large flat surface in the order shown on the Layout Drawing. Using a ½-inch seam allowance and alternating the embroidered squares with the 8-inch lattice strips, join the squares into six strips. Trim the seams to ¼ inch and press them toward the blue.

Beginning with a strip of squares, join the six strips to the five 3 × 37-inch pieces. Trim the seams and press. Stitch the two 4 × 37-inch blue strips to the top and bottom edges of the piece. Trim the seams and press.

Finally, sew the two 4 × 61-inch pieces to the sides. Trim the seams and press.

The Crazy Quilt Embroidery

Embroider one of the Crazy Quilt designs around each square. Work right over the seam, centering the design over it. The seam is shown as a dashed line on the sides of the embroidery diagrams to help with placement.

The numbers in the blocks in the Layout Drawing correspond to the numbers of the bird motifs. If you wish to distribute the patterns of the stitching evenly over the quilt, always use the matching number Crazy Quilt embroidery pattern with the indicated bird squares.

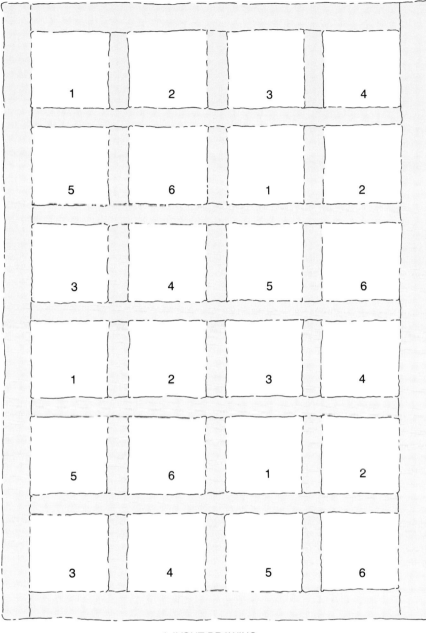

LAYOUT DRAWING

Two additional stitch patterns are included for extra variety if desired. By varying the colors and mixing up the embroidery stitching patterns, you can make it appear that each square has a different design stitched around it.

Do the Crazy Quilt stitching with two strands of embroidery floss and the #7 crewel needle.

MOTIF 1

MOTIF 2

MOTIF 3

56

MOTIF 4

MOTIF 5

MOTIF 6

Embroidery Pattern 1

Outline the square with a row of pink chain stitches worked directly on the seam. Make the stitches about ⅛ inch long. From the middle of each chain make a green straight stitch ¼ inch long slanting out at about a 45-degree angle. Alternate these last stitches to slant first from one side, then the other, as shown on the drawing. Place a blue French knot at the end of each slanting stitch.

Embroidery Pattern 2

Place a row of yellow French knots on the seam, making them about ½ inch apart. With green floss, make long straight stitches lying on the seam and connecting the French knots. Work a cluster of three lazy daisy stitches at each French knot, placing them alternately on the blue and the white fabric as shown on the drawing. Alternate the thread color also, using pink on the blue, blue on the white.

Embroidery Pattern 3

Place a row of green French knots on the seam, making them ½ inch apart. With pink thread, make two lazy daisy stitches perpendicular to the seam at each French knot. Using yellow, make a small straight stitch—about ⅛ inch long—on the blue side of the seam halfway between the lazy daisy stitches. With blue thread, make a series of slanting stitches on the white side of the seam, placing them as shown on the drawing.

Embroidery Pattern 4

With yellow thread, work a row of straight stitches around the square, making the stitches ¼ inch long and placing them right on the seam. On the blue side of the seam, use pink thread to work clusters of three straight stitches placed in a fan shape at the end of every alternate yellow stitch. Using blue thread, repeat the clusters on the white fabric in the remaining spaces.

Embroidery Pattern 5

With yellow thread, place a row of French knots on the seam, leaving about ½ inch between them. Using pink floss, make fan-shaped clusters of three lazy daisy petals at alternate French knots on the white side of the seam. Place a single blue lazy daisy stitch perpendicular to the seam at the other French knots. Make a zigzag row of green straight stitches on the blue side of the seam as shown on the drawing.

Embroidery Pattern 6

Make a row of yellow French knots on the seam, placing them ½ inch apart. Connect the French knots with a line of green straight stitches also lying on the seam. With pink thread, make a cross-stitch and a long vertical stitch centered over the green straight stitch. Also with the pink, make a short horizontal stitch across the latter group of three stitches at the point at which they cross.

Embroidery Pattern 7

Work a row of pink feather stitches, centering them over the seam. On the blue side of the seam, work a yellow French knot at the end of each arm of the feather stitch. Make a green French knot at the end of the stitches on the white side of the seam.

Embroidery Pattern 8

Center a row of blue feather stitches over the seam. Make a yellow lazy daisy stitch over the arm of each feather stitch on the blue fabric. Repeat with a green lazy daisy stitch over each arm on the white side of the seam.

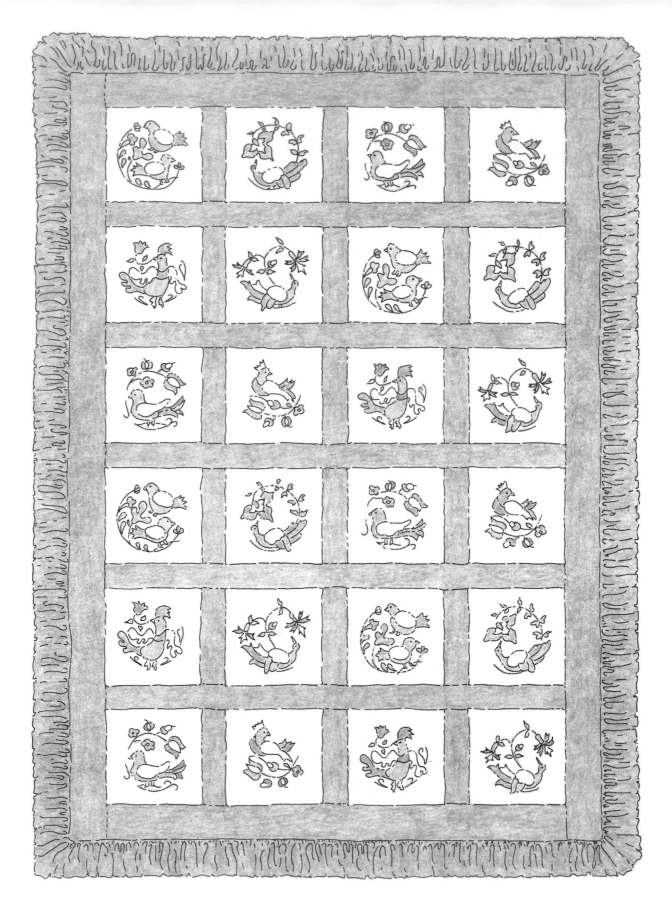

Finishing the Quilt

Make the quilt ruffle by joining the 7-inch-wide strips into a continuous 14-yard piece. Fold through the middle, bringing raw edges together to make a double ruffle 3½ inches wide. Pin the raw edges together. Place two rows of machine stitching along the raw edge, with the first ¼ inch from the edge, the second ⅛ inch inside the first. Pull up the bobbin threads to make the ruffle fit the outside edges of the quilt top.

Check to make certain the borders on all four sides are the same width. If not, trim them. Pin the ruffle to the right side of the quilt top, with the raw edges matching the raw edges of the quilt top. Place extra fullness at the four corners so the ruffle will lie flat. Stitch the two together.

Press the quilt top well, applying the iron only to the wrong side. Layer the quilt backing, the batting, and the embroidered top. Pin them securely.

At the corners of the squares, tie the three layers together. To make the ties, use three strands of blue embroidery floss in the #7 crewel needle. Enter the quilt from the back, leaving a 3-inch tail of thread. Make three stitches on top of one another, finishing on the back. Tie the threads in a secure knot. Thread the ends into the needle and bury them in the quilt batting.

Check to make certain the backing and batting are even with the quilt top. If not, trim them. Turn the raw edges to the inside and stitch them to close with small invisible stitches.

The Sweet Dreams Pillow

Finished size: 12″ × 12″ exclusive of the ruffle

Construction

Mark and embroider the white batiste square to match one square of the comforter. Wash to remove any remaining markings. Baste the lining to the embroidered square.

Taking a ½ inch seam, stitch the two 8-inch blue strips to the sides of the square. Sew the two 13-inch strips to the top and bottom of the piece. Trim the seams and press them toward the blue.

Seam the ruffle strips to make a continuous piece. Fold in half lengthwise to make a 3¼-inch-wide double ruffle. Pin the cut edges together. Gather the ruffle to fit the outside edges of the pillow top.

Pin the ruffle to the right side of the pillow top, matching the raw edges. Allow extra fullness at the corners so the ruffle will lie flat. Baste in place.

With the right sides together, seam the pillow top to the backing, joining in the ruffle and leaving an opening for turning and stuffing. Trim the corners and turn. Fill evenly with fiberfill. Close the seam with small invisible stitches.

Materials for One Pillow

Pale blue broadcloth, poly-cotton blend, 42″ wide—1 yard
White batiste, poly-cotton blend—one piece 8″ × 8″
White lining fabric—one piece 8″ × 8″
Embroidery thread to match quilt—one skein each color
Polyester fiberfill—slightly less than 1 pound

Cutting Guide

From the blue broadcloth cut:
    1 square 13 × 13 inches for pillow back
    2 pieces 3½ × 8 inches
    2 pieces 3½ × 13 inches
    Enough 6½-inch-wide strips to piece together a 3½-yard ruffle

VICTORIA

A PINK AND WHITE HEIRLOOM
Finished size: 30″ × 39″ exclusive of ruffle

THE PROSPECTS OF A NEW BABY GIRL entice us to visions of ruffles, lace, and ribbons. This little quilt will satisfy any quilter's urge to create the sweetest confection ever for that little one. The white center panel stenciled with a profusion of pink ribbon bows is a pretty foil for the elegant Victorian puffing border and wide Swiss embroidered ruffle. The bassinette or stroller dressed with this silky cotton cover will be a delight to all.

Puffing, a traditional Victorian fabric embellishment, is a narrow strip of fabric—usually about 2½ inches wide—that is gathered on both sides. The gathers are arranged so the folds lie in parallel rows, and the edges are stabilized by stitching them to entredeux, which is the hallmark of Victorian or heirloom sewing. It lends a beautiful texture and depth to clothing and linens.

As shown, the quilt is a small size most suitable for a newborn, but it can be altered easily to full crib size. To make a larger quilt, simply increase the dimensions and either repeat the stencil pattern more often or trace the stencil pattern and enlarge it slightly by copier. An enlargement to 125 percent of the original would increase the distance from bow knot to bow knot from 4 inches to 5 inches.

Materials
Pale pink Swiss batiste, 100%
cotton, 44″ wide—2¾ yards
White Swiss batiste, 100% cotton,
44″ wide—2½ yards
White Swiss eyelet beading,
1⅛″ wide—4½ yards

Finding the Materials
This Swiss batiste is sheer and smooth. When finished, the little quilt is cloud soft and light as a feather. If you decide to substitute a poly-blend batiste, check the label of the stencil paint to ascertain that it will be permanent on the blended fiber fabric.

The above yardage requirements assume that it will be necessary to use a double layer of white batiste for the quilt top to prevent the batting from

White Swiss eyelet edging,
  6″ wide—9 yards
Pale pink double-faced satin
  ribbon, 1″ wide—5⅝ yards
White entredeux—7 yards
Polyester quilting fleece—crib size
Pale pink stencil paint
Stencil film—3 sheets 9″ × 12″
#50 white cotton mercerized
  sewing thread for quilting
#60 white cotton mercerized
  sewing thread for construction

Cutting Guide

From the white batiste cut:
  1 piece 21 × 30 inches for the
  stenciled panel
  1 piece 33 × 41 inches for the
  quilt top lining
From the pink batiste cut:
  1 piece 33 × 41 inches for the
  quilt back
  12 strips 2¾ × 44 inches
  4 strips 2¾ × 22 inches
  4 pieces 5½ × 6 inches for
  corner extensions
From the eyelet beading cut:
  2 pieces 41 inches long
  2 pieces 33 inches long
From the entredeux cut:
  2 strips 41 inches long
  2 strips 29¾ inches long
  2 pieces 20¾ inches long
  2 pieces 33 inches long

showing through and lending a grayish cast to the quilt. If your fabric is a bit heavier than the Swiss, you need only half the white yardage.

A lightweight polyester quilt batting such as those labeled Classic or Traditional can be substituted for the fleece.

As you can see from the photo, entredeux—a French word that means "between two"—is a narrow strip of little embroidered holes with batiste edging. It is pretty but also functional and necessary when making the puffing borders. Notice also that both edges of the beading piece are finished with the little entredeux holes.

Before you begin working, check the Basic Sewing Supplies list on page 11, the Basic Quilting Supplies list on page 12, and the Stenciling Supplies list on page 26 to make sure you have everything you will need on hand.

Stenciling

Stencil the smaller of the white batiste pieces, setting aside the larger one as noted for the lining for the top.

A stencil is the ideal tool for laying out the grid on which to stencil while leaving only the smallest of marks. To lay out the grid pattern, draw a line across the top of a sheet of stencil film 1½ inches down from the top edge. Place the film over the drawing of the Bow Motif and mark the five small dots—three at the centers of the bows, two below the ends of the lower ribbons. Cut a little round hole at each dot on the film.

If you look at the color drawing of the quilt, you will notice that across the top of the stenciled panel there are four full bows as well as one half bow on each side. Place the stencil film on the fabric panel with the straight edge at the top on the cut edge of the fabric and the first hole 1 inch from the side edge of the panel as shown by the pink area on Figure 1. Make the lightest possible mark at the five openings. (Use a 4H pencil rather than a washout pen for these marks, and before stenciling make a test sample to check to be certain the marks will not show through the stencil paint. If they do, erase them partially with a cloth eraser so they are very faint.)

Move the stencil to the right so the two openings at the left side line up with the two marks made on the panel at the right side and mark the next three dots. Continue moving the stencil, using previous dots as reference points, until the panel is marked to correspond to Figure 1.

Although only one color stencil paint is used for the pink ribbons, it is necessary to cut two stencils—one for each shade of pink shown on the Bow Motif.

Use the stencil shown as the lighter pink first, centering the knots over the dots on the fabric.

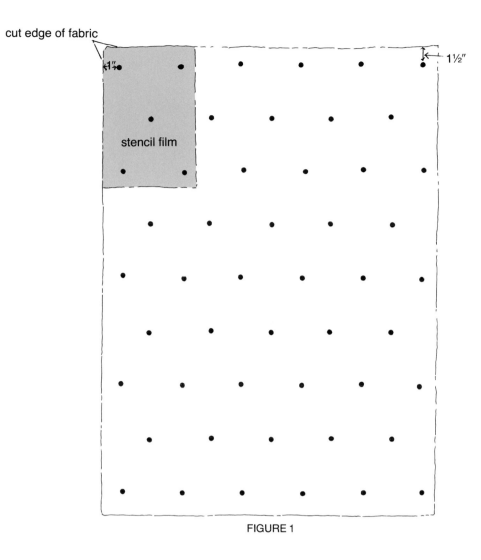

cut edge of fabric

stencil film

1″

1½″

FIGURE 1

Follow with the second stencil, completing the bow design. When the paint is dry, set it according to the manufacturer's directions. Press the piece if necessary.

Assembly and Quilting

Place the pink quilt back on a flat surface. Layer the quilt batting on top and smooth out any bubbles. Place the white lining piece on top of the batting. Next, center the stenciled panel on top of the lining. Pin the layers together securely and baste.

With white #50 cotton thread, quilt the outlines of the stenciled bows, placing the stitches on the white fabric against the pink outlines of the pattern. *Leave several inches unquilted around the four edges of the panel so the beading can be seamed to the quilt top later.*

BOW MOTIF

Finishing

After the quilting—except for the edges—has been completed, remove the basting threads so the batting, lining, and backing can be held back from the stenciled panel. Trim the quilted panel so it is ½ inch wider and longer than the stenciled area.

Puffing Borders

Make the four border pieces next.

To make the puffing for the long sides, stitch two of the 2¾ × 44-inch pink batiste strips together to make a piece 87 inches long. Place two rows of gathering stitches ¼ inch apart along each of the two edges. Pull up the bobbin threads to gather the piece to measure 29¾ inches long. Distribute the gathers evenly. Mark the center.

Fold one of the 29¾-inch strips of entredeux in half and mark the middle. Pin one gathered edge of the batiste puffing to the entredeux, right sides together and matching the centers and the raw edges. Stitch the two together, placing the stitching as close as possible to the embroidery of the entredeux.

Without touching the gathered batiste with the iron, press the seam and trim it to ¼ inch. Press the seam allowance toward the batiste.

Seam two more of the 44-inch pink batiste strips together and repeat the four gathering rows. Pull up the bobbin threads so the piece is 29¾ inches long. Stitch one side to the entredeux on the puffing strip. Trim the seam and press it toward the batiste.

At each end of the puffing, stitch one of the 5½ × 6-inch pink corner extension pieces.

Stitch one of the 41-inch long pieces of entredeux to one side of the piece. On the other side stitch a 41-inch long piece of beading. Use the entredeux edging of the beading just as the narrow entredeux was used, placing the seam stitching at the edge of the embroidery. The piece will look like Figure 2.

Repeat the above steps for the other long side border.

Mark the centers of the stenciled panel sides and the border pieces. Holding the backing, batting, and lining out of the way, stitch the puffing borders to

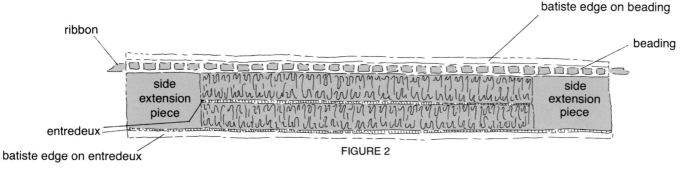

FIGURE 2

the long sides of the stenciled panels. The borders should extend beyond the ends of the panel to the edges of the lining and backing. Leave the extended ends unstitched.

To make the puffing for the short sides—the top and bottom—stitch one 44-inch strip to one 22-inch strip. Repeat the four gathering rows. Pull up the bobbin threads to gather the strip to fit one 20¾-inch piece of entredeux. Stitch the entredeux to one side of the gathered strip. Press the seam and trim it. Press the raw edges toward the batiste.

Make and gather a second 66-inch puffing strip to 20¾ inches. Stitch one side of it to the entredeux just attached to the first piece. Stitch a 33-inch strip of beading to one side of the piece.

Repeat the above steps for the other short border.

Mark the centers of the beading and the short sides of the panel. Leaving the seams unstitched ½ inch at each end, stitch the beading to the panel. Allow the beading to lie on top of the vertical borders and tuck the ends of the puffing under the beading of those borders. Press the batiste edges of the beading to the wrong side. Pin the pieces in place on the lining only.

Weave the ribbon through the beading. Pin it so it stays in place.

Still holding the backing and the batting out of the way, stitch the beading extensions in place with a very tiny zigzag stitch.

Trim the edges of the three layers even, if necessary. Stitch a strip of entredeux to the short outside edges, allowing the beading to extend into the seam.

On a small piece of paper trace one bow from the stencil design. Slide the paper between the layers under the four corner blocks and trace one bow in each corner. Quilt the bows and also stitch a row of quilting ¼ inch inside the blocks. Finish the quilting along the edges of the stenciled panel.

Ruffle

Gather the eyelet ruffle to fit the outside edge of the quilt. With right sides together, stitch the eyelet to the batiste edge of the entredeux on the sides of the quilt. Add extra fullness at the corners so the ruffle will lie flat. Press the seam and trim it to ⅛ inch.

Set the machine for a zigzag stitch the same width as the trimmed seam. Place the seam under the presser foot so the stitches enter the batiste on the seam line and go off the edge on the other side. Zigzag the seam to finish it. Press it toward the ruffle.

Turn the backing and batting to the inside along the edge of the entredeux on the back and whipstitch the edges closed to finish the quilt.

Make a bow from the remaining ribbon and sew it to the ribbon in the beading at the top of the quilt as shown in the quilt drawing.

ANTIQUE HEARTS

A NEW "ANTIQUE" FOR A DOLL BED
Finished size: 27½" × 27½"

COLLECTORS OF ANTIQUE DOLL QUILTS love this old pattern, which apparently was a favorite among early quiltmakers. Though sometimes made from calico scraps appliquéd to the background and sometimes stenciled, as was this one, they all are charming. One feature that I have borrowed from a favorite of mine is an odd heart— one gold one mixed in with fifteen blue ones. It is a nice surprise—an unassuming folk art touch we find appealing.

The sizes of antique doll quilts vary so much that it is hard to make one the standard. This one was made to fit an old doll bed and is square. The pattern would be easy to change to a rectangle or make larger or smaller simply by changing the number and arrangement of the stenciled squares.

Because it was going to be used on the antique doll bed, the quilt in the photograph has been "antiqued" by a coffee solution painted on along the seam lines. This is an easy way to make the little quilt fit in perfectly as a small wall hanging or table cover in a country room.

Finding the Materials

These old-looking calicos are easy to find and add an authentic "antique" feel to little quilts like this. The striped patterns in both lend a pretty touch, but floral calicos would also be pretty. Choose all-cotton fabrics if you intend to apply the coffee or tea antiquing solution, as this fiber takes the color best.

Choose the blue stencil paint to coordinate with the blue fabric frame around the field of hearts. The colors used for this quilt were named Colonial Blue and Colonial Gold. Both are softly grayed to old-looking shades.

Before you begin working, check the Basic Sewing Supplies list on page 11, the Basic Quilting Supplies list on page 12, and the Stenciling Supplies list on page 26 to make sure you have everything you will need on hand.

Materials

Natural muslin, 100% cotton, 42" wide—1¾ yards
Dark blue calico stripe, 100% cotton, 42" wide—¾ yard
Light calico print on natural background, 100% cotton, 42" wide—¾ yard
Traditional quilt batting— 28" × 28"
#50 off-white cotton mercerized thread for piecing and quilting
Stencil paint or crayons— blue and gold
Stencil film—6" × 6"

Cutting Guide

From the muslin cut:
  The quilt backing, 29 × 29
  inches
  16 squares 4½ × 4½ inches
  (Heart Template) (See
  Stenciling, *right,* before cutting
  these.)
From the blue calico cut:
  4 pieces 2½ × 19 inches
  Enough 1½-inch bias strips to
  piece to a length of 116 inches
From the light calico print cut:
  4 pieces 5¼ × 29 inches

Stenciling

If this is your first stenciling on fabric project, please read the basic instructions on page 26 before beginning.

  Use the heart template for both the muslin squares and the stenciling design. Carefully trace the outline of the square and the heart onto the stencil film. Cut on the outlines to make a template for cutting the muslin squares and a stencil for the hearts.

HEART TEMPLATE

Place the template on the muslin and draw sixteen squares, using the outside edge of the film as the guide. Do not cut out the squares until *after* the stenciling is complete.

Following the instructions, with your paint or crayon stencil fifteen blue hearts and one gold heart. This quilt looks older if the paint is applied more heavily at the edges of the hearts and some little bit of the center area is left natural. Set the paint as the manufacturer suggests. Cut out the squares.

Assembling the Top

In this quilt, the single gold heart was placed in the lower left corner. Place yours wherever it pleases you.

Taking up a ¼-inch seam allowance, stitch the squares into four rows of four hearts each. Trim the seams and press. Matching the seam lines, stitch the four rows into one piece. Trim the seams and press.

Stitch the four 19-inch blue border pieces to the top, bottom, and sides of the piece, leaving the width of the seam allowance unstitched at both ends of each piece. Fold the tails to miter the corners so the stripes appear to turn the corners in a frame. Stitch the corner seams. Trim the seams and press.

Following the same procedure as for the blue borders, stitch the 29-inch light calico border pieces to the blue and miter the corners. Trim the seams and press.

Antiquing and Assembling the Quilt

Following the instructions for antiquing on page 23, tint the pieced top. Immerse it first in water so the dye will bleed evenly into the fabric. Use a watercolor brush and paint the solution along all the seam lines, including those in the borders. Iron dry. If not enough color remains after the piece is dry, repeat the process where needed.

While you have the coffee or tea solution at hand, wet and dip the fabric for the backing and binding so they are also "aged."

Layer the quilt backing, the batting, and the pieced top. Smooth out any wrinkles. Pin or baste securely so the layers won't shift during the quilting.

Quilting

To enhance the old look, quilt by hand, unless time is very short and the speed provided by a machine is necessary.

Quilt around each stenciled heart, placing the stitching on the muslin just outside the edges of color. Quilt on each seam line, placing the stitches "in the ditch." Quilt also ¼ inch inside each square.

When all quilting has been finished, trim the outside edges even and bind them with blue following the instructions for bias binding on page 23. Quilt another line of stitches ¼ inch inside the binding.

STRIPES AND STARS

BOLD COLOR AND DESIGN FOR THE CRIB
Finished size: 40½″ × 49½″

THIS IS A QUICK LITTLE QUILT, MADE employing the quilt-as-you-go method. It provides a warm and fluffy spark of color for any nursery! The bright red and white stripes are very graphic, but a totally different look can be made using pastel colors or a combination of white and small prints. This quilt is fun and easy to make. The method of stitching the stripes to the backing to create the quilting is intriguing.

Finding the Materials
Color is the most important factor in this quilt. Look for a good-quality red fabric—it can be any smooth material. If a good red cotton is not to be found, or if you prefer it, use one of the poly-blend broadcloths. They are fine for this quilt, producing a soft, silky feel we like for baby things.

Check the red carefully when washing to be certain it is colorfast. If there is any bleeding, let it stand overnight in a solution containing water, white vinegar, and salt. Rinse the fabric well and iron dry.

The fluffy extra-loft batting works well in this quilt-as-you-go method and produces a puffy comforter-type quilt that will be warm and snuggly.

Before shopping for materials, check the Basic Sewing Supplies list on page 11 to make sure you have everything you will need on hand.

Materials
White cotton broadcloth or
    muslin, 42″ wide—3 yards
Red cotton broadcloth or sateen,
    42″ wide—½ yard
Red and white striped cotton,
    42″ wide—¾ yard
Extra-loft batting—42″ × 54″
Fusible thread
#50 red cotton thread for appliqué
Transparent nylon quilting thread
#30 white cotton cord for
    piping—20 yards
Hot-iron transfer pencil

Cutting Guide

Cut from the white fabric:
    The quilt backing, 42 × 54
    inches
    2 horizontal borders 6 × 42
    inches
    2 vertical borders 6 × 42½
    inches
    4 vertical stripes 3¾ × 42½
    inches

Cut from the red and white striped
    fabric:
    20 yards bias strips 1¼ inches
    wide

Cut from the red fabric:
    5 vertical stripes 4½ × 42½
    inches
    Reserve remaining for 22 stars

Assembly

Place the quilt back on a flat surface and spread the batting on top. Pin the two together and baste them with rows about 1½ inches apart.

Following the instructions on page 22, make 20 yards of corded piping using the red and white striped bias strips.

Trace the star and, using a hot-iron transfer pencil, make a pattern. Iron twenty-two stars on the red fabric. Do not cut out the stars. Place fusible thread in the bobbin of the sewing machine and red thread on the top. Using a short straight stitch—about ten to the inch or 2 mm—stitch exactly on the outline of the stars.

Cut the stars apart just outside the stitching line.

Draw a light line vertically through the middle of the two 6 × 42½-inch vertical border pieces. Find the center of this line—21¼ inches down from the top—and mark it. Place one star over the center mark so the points of the star marked A and B on the drawing are exactly on the line to center it as shown in Figure 1. Pin the star in place.

Measure up from the tip of the star (A) 4⅞ inches and place another star with point B on the center line at the 4⅞-inch mark. Pin the star in position. Measure up 4⅞ inches again and pin a third star in place. Measure down from the first star and position two more stars. The piece will look like Figure 1.

A

B

STAR TEMPLATE

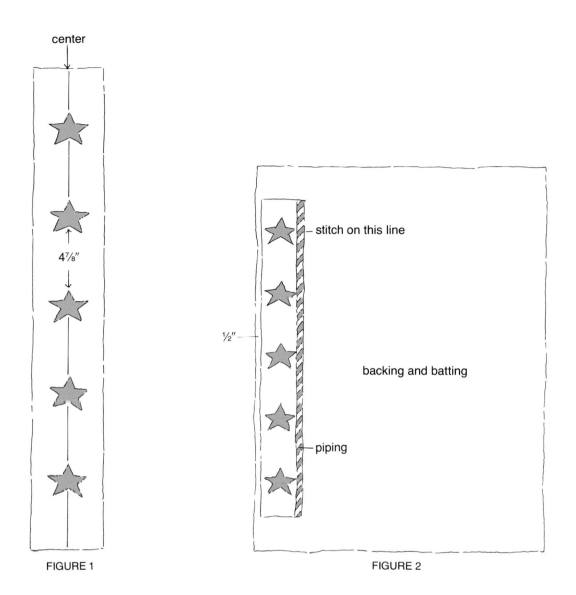

center

$4\frac{7}{8}''$

FIGURE 1

stitch on this line

$\frac{1}{2}''$

backing and batting

piping

FIGURE 2

Repeat for the other vertical border.

Iron the stars, fusing the thread to attach them. Using a zigzag stitch and red thread, appliqué the stars to the borders, placing the stitching so that the stitches cover the raw edges of the stars.

Matching the raw edges of the 42½-inch length, stitch a piece of piping to the right side of one of the star-trimmed vertical borders.

To begin construction and quilting, place the backing and batting on a large flat surface, with the batting on top. Pin the piped border right side up to one side, leaving about ½ inch on the outside and dividing the extra length of the backing and batting between the two ends. Pin the border to the backing and batting as shown in Figure 2.

Matching the raw edges, stitch a piece of piping to one of the 42½-inch-long sides of a red stripe. With right sides together, pin the plain edge of this

strip over the piping on the border piece. Stitch through all layers. Flip the red strip so its right side is up, and pin the piped edge to the batting.

Following this procedure, always stitching through all layers and stitching piping to one edge, alternate red and white stripes. Stitch all stripes and the second border piece to the backing and batting piece.

Stitch a piece of piping across one long side of each horizontal border. Lay the quilt out flat and place the borders to establish the placement of the stars on these pieces. These stars should be centered over the white stripes, with the two end ones centered over those on the vertical borders. Pin the stars in place, iron them to fuse the thread, then zigzag to appliqué.

Pin the piped side of the horizontal borders to the batting to cover the raw edges of the stripes. Lift the border fabric from the batting at each end, and stitch the borders together along the piping line for about an inch. Pin them back in place and then stitch the end borders through all thicknesses, but begin and end the stitching 1 inch from the ends. This leaves the ends free so the outside piping can be attached to the quilt top.

If the stripes extend above the seam line into the border and can be seen through it, carefully rip the stitches holding them back to the seam line and trim the stripes even with the seam.

Trim the edges of the three layers evenly. Holding the borders free of the batting and backing, stitch piping around the entire outside of the quilt. Begin and end at the middle of the bottom

Turn the raw edges to the inside and whipstitch them together along the seam line. Remove the basting threads visible on the back of the quilt.

Using transparent nylon quilting thread, quilt around the outline of the stars, placing the stitches just outside the red appliqué stitching.

CALICO SURPRISE

A TINY CHARMER
Finished size: 17½″ × 21¾″

Finding the Materials

The pieces from which the main portion of this little quilt was stitched were purchased in a package all neatly die-cut to perfect 2-inch squares. This is a good way to obtain the variety that adds so much to the overall charm of this kind of little quilt. If you have a wonderful collection of small pieces of fabric, you could cut your own.

Before you begin working, check the Basic Sewing Supplies list on page 11 and the Basic Quilting Supplies list on page 12 to make sure you have everything you will need on hand.

Assembly

Join the eighty-eight squares into eleven rows of eight squares each, mixing the colors and patterns any way that looks pretty to you. Trim the seams to ⅛ inch and press well.

Join the rows to make a piece measuring 11¾ × 16 inches. Trim the seams and press.

Stitch the two 16-inch yellow calico strips to the sides of the piece. Next stitch the two 13-inch yellow strips to the top and bottom of the piece. Trim the seams and press.

Stitch the two 17-inch navy border strips to the sides of the piece. Trim the seams and press. Stitch the remaining two navy border pieces to the top and bottom. Trim the seams and press.

Layer the red quilt backing, the batting, and the quilt top, smoothing out all wrinkles. Pin securely.

Quilt the pieced field "in the ditch" of all seams. Stitch similarly around the yellow borders. Quilt on the navy border ½ inch from the yellow border.

Trim the three layers to the same length. Turn the raw edges to the inside and whipstitch them together. Quilt again ½ inch from the edge of the quilt.

Materials

88 100% cotton calico squares, 2″ × 2″
Yellow floral calico, 100% cotton, 42″ wide—4″ × 16″
Red geometric calico, 100% cotton, 42″ wide—19″ × 23″
Navy 100% cotton, 42″ wide— ¼ yard
Traditional quilt batting— 19″ × 23″
Transparent nylon quilting thread
#50 off-white cotton mercerized thread for piecing

Cutting Guide

From the yellow calico cut:
    2 strips 1 × 16 inches
    2 strips 1 × 13 inches
From the navy cut:
    2 pieces 3½ × 17 inches
    2 pieces 3½ × 19 inches

LUCKY STARS

AN UPDATED OHIO STAR FOR THE NURSERY
Finished size: 40″ × 48″

Materials

White-on-white print, 100%
   cotton, 42″ wide—2 yards
Blue and white plaid (#1), 100%
   cotton, 42″ wide—2⅛ yards
Dark maroon plaid (#2), 100%
   cotton, 45″ wide—½ yard
Medium blue ombre stripe (#3),
   100% cotton, 45″ wide—
   ¼ yard
Medium blue plaid (#4), 100%
   cotton, 45″ wide—⅛ yard
Medium blue plaid (#5), 100%
   cotton, 45″ wide—⅛ yard
White and blue plaid (#6), 100%
   cotton, 45″ wide—⅛ yard
Traditional quilt batting—crib size
#50 white cotton mercerized
   thread for piecing and quilting

Finding the Materials

Except for the background white-on-white print, the materials in this quilt are from a collection of stripes and plaids designed to be used together. These are found in quilt shops and do make selecting fabric easier. To help you select other fabrics, the following is a brief description of the plaids and stripes used: #1, which is used as borders and backing as well as part of the pieced design, is a white background with an open window-pane type plaid in medium and dark blue. #2 is a very deep, rich maroon plaid with very fine blue and white lines. #3 is an ombre stripe in medium blue on a lighter background. #4 is another window-pane plaid of deep blue on a medium blue background. #5 is a Glen plaid stripe of navy on a chambray-like background. #6 is a white background with a navy blue narrow-line open plaid.

The white-on-white print is a very subtle floral that adds just a bit of texture to the background areas. If not available, substitute a plain white cotton.

You may wish to assort your plaids and stripes differently. To help with that, the pieces needed for one Ohio Star are listed with the instructions for constructing one block. In addition, each star block on the drawing of the quilt has been numbered, and a list explaining the combination of plaids in each square is included in the directions under To Construct the Star Block.

Before you begin working, check the Basic Sewing Supplies list on page 11 and the Basic Quilting Supplies list on page 12 to make sure you have everything you will need on hand.

Cutting Guide

From blue and white plaid (#1)
cut:

The quilt backing, 42 × 50
inches

2 borders 5 × 37½ inches

2 borders 5 × 29 inches

2 squares 3½ × 3½ inches
(Template 1)

1 square 2¾ × 2¾ inches
(Template 2)

From white-on-white print cut:

2 borders 1 × 36 inches

2 borders 1 × 29½ inches

2 outside borders 2½ × 46
inches

2 outside borders 2½ × 41
inches

31 lattice strips 2 × 7¼ inches

24 squares 3½ × 3½ inches
(Template 1)

58 squares 2¾ × 2¾ inches
(Template 2)

From maroon plaid (#2) cut:

6 squares 3½ × 3½ inches
(Template 1)

10 squares 2¾ × 2¾ inches
(Template 2)

From blue ombre stripe
(#3) cut:

6 squares 3½ × 3½ inches
(Template 1)

10 squares 2¾ × 2¾ inches
(Template 2)

From blue plaid (#4) cut:

4 squares 3½ × 3½ inches
(Template 1)

1 square 2¾ × 2¾ inches
(Template 2)

From blue plaid (#5) cut:

4 squares 3½ × 3½ inches
(Template 1)

1 square 2¾ × 2¾ inches
(Template 2)

From white and blue plaid (#6)
cut:

2 squares 3½ × 3½ inches
(Template 1)

TEMPLATE 1

TEMPLATE 2

To Assemble One Block

Each Ohio Star block is made up of nine small squares. The four squares that compose the star points are each constructed from four triangles. Figure 1 shows one complete square.

Making this quilt requires twelve large blocks and four smaller corner blocks. The quick construction method that follows simplifies the process and at the same time perfects it by eliminating the need to sew the bias sides of the little triangles together.

The pieces needed for one block like #3 on the quilt drawing—with the blue ombre striped center and maroon points—are:

2 white 3½ × 3½-inch squares (Template 1)
2 maroon 3½ × 3½-inch squares (Template 1)
1 medium blue ombre 2¾ × 2¾-inch square (Template 2)
4 white 2¾ × 2¾-inch squares (Template 2)

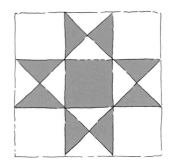

FIGURE 1
One Complete Ohio Star Block

The Star Points

Step 1: Draw a diagonal line on the wrong side of one 3½-inch white square.

With right sides together, stitch one white 3½-inch square to one maroon square of the same size, placing the lines of stitching ¼ inch on either side of the drawn diagonal as shown in the illustration.

Step 2: Cut apart on the drawn diagonal line. Unfold the resulting bicolor squares and press the seam allowance toward the darker fabric as shown in the illustration below.

Step 3: With right sides together, place two bicolor squares together so that the white triangle of one is against the maroon triangle of the other. Draw a diagonal line from corner to corner and perpendicular to the seam line. Stitch on either side of the line as shown. Cut through the drawn line and press.

Step 4: The finished star point will look like the drawing for Step 4 and measure 2¾ × 2¾ inches. This process created two star points. Repeat to make one more set.

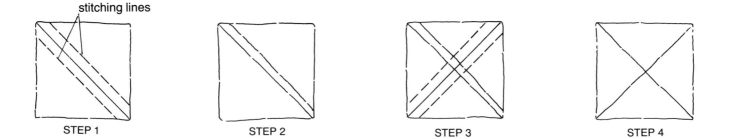

stitching lines

STEP 1   STEP 2   STEP 3   STEP 4

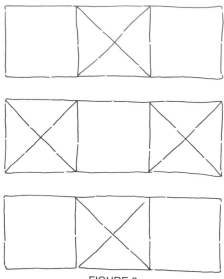

FIGURE 2

To Construct the Star Block

Using the medium blue ombre square as the center and the four white 2¾-inch squares as the corners, stitch the nine pieces together as shown in Figure 2 to create one Ohio Star block. Noting the placement of the star points, first stitch together the three rows of squares. Then stitch the rows together to form the square.

Construct twelve Ohio Star blocks in an assortment of colors and plaids. Note that each block on the quilt drawing has been numbered. To assemble your quilt exactly like the pictured one, make the following blocks:

Block 1—points #1 blue; center #2 maroon
Block 2—points #3 blue; center #2 maroon
Block 3—points #2 maroon; center #3. blue
Block 4—points #4 blue; center #2 maroon
Block 5—points #5 white plaid; center #3 blue
Block 6—points #3 blue; center #3 blue
Block 7—points #5 blue, center #4 blue
Block 8—points #2 maroon; center #3 blue
Block 9—points #4 blue; center #2 maroon
Block 10—points #3 blue; center #2 maroon
Block 11—points #5 blue; center #1 blue
Block 12—points #2 maroon; center #5 blue

To Construct Lattice Blocks

For the twenty lattice blocks, pick out from the cut 2¾-inch squares ten white print, five maroon plaid, and five blue ombre striped.

To construct the lattice blocks, use the same stitching and cutting methods as for the star points, working as follows: Stitch one white square to one maroon square, one blue square to one white square. After cutting them apart and pressing, match one blue and white to one maroon and white, stitch, and cut apart to make a three-color block. The finished blocks should measure 2 × 2 inches.

Assembling the Quilt Top

Lay the twelve star blocks on a flat surface and arrange them in four rows of three each, matching the layout on the color drawing of the quilt. Beginning and ending with lattice strips, join three blocks and four white lattice strips into the four crosswise rows.

Beginning and ending with the three-color lattice blocks, join four lattice blocks and three lattice strips into a long lattice strip. Make five such strips.

Beginning and ending with long lattice strips, join the rows of blocks into one piece. Trim the seams and press.

Stitch the longer maroon borders to the long sides of the pieced top. Trim the seams and press the allowance toward the maroon. Stitch the other two maroon strips to the top and bottom of the piece. Trim and press.

Stitch the longer 1-inch-wide white border strips to the long sides of the quilt top. Stitch the two shorter strips to the top and bottom. Trim seams and press.

Miniature Ohio Star Corner Blocks

The pieces for these miniature blocks have not yet been cut.
For each miniature corner block cut:

　　2 white squares 2¾ × 2¾ inches (Template 2)
　　1 maroon square 2¾ × 2¾ inches (Template 2)
　　1 blue square 2¾ × 2¾ inches (Template 2)
　　1 white 2-inch square (Template 3)
　　4 blue 2-inch squares (Template 3)

Although there is plenty of fabric left for you to mix the color combinations as you like in these little blocks, you will note that on our quilt blue has been used in all four corner blocks to assure an even coloring.

Stitch the squares cut from Template 2 as for lattice blocks to make three-color star points. Assemble the blocks following the method for making the larger blocks. These smaller blocks measure 5 × 5 inches.

TEMPLATE 3

Borders

Stitch the longer of the plaid border pieces to the long sides of the quilt. Trim the seam and press.

Assemble the top and bottom borders by stitching a miniature corner block to both ends of each 29-inch plaid strip. Stitch the strips to the top and bottom of the quilt top. Trim the seams and press.

Stitch the two longer white outside border pieces to the sides of the piece. Then stitch the remaining two white borders to the top and bottom. Trim the seams and press.

Assembling the Quilt

Press both the quilt top and the backing well. Layer the plaid backing, the batting, and the finished quilt top, carefully smoothing out any wrinkles. Pin securely, then baste the layers together, placing the rows of basting about 2 inches apart.

Quilt by hand or machine with white thread. Place the quilting "in the ditch" around all pieces, then inside the lattice strips and corner squares as shown on the Quilting Guide. Quilt also the white outside border ½ inch outside the blue plaid border.

When all quilting has been finished, trim the outside edges evenly. Trim the batting another ¼ inch. Turn the raw edges to the inside and whipstitch them closed. Quilt again ½ inch from the edge of the quilt.

QUILTING GUIDE

POSTAGE STAMP STRIPE

A MINIATURE PIECED DOLL QUILT
Finished size: 15″ × 17″ exclusive of 2″ ruffle

THIS IS A CUTE DOLL QUILT WITH AN appealing country theme adapted from an old quilt pattern. Most often made from scraps, the postage stamp design is an easy one to reduce to a scale appropriate for a doll quilt. You probably have more than enough remnants of fabric on hand to construct the stripes for this little treasure.

Finding the Materials

The off-white basic print for this quilt is one of the new, easy to find quilters' prints. It has a tiny coffee-colored triangle formed by three dots scattered over it. Any of the small geometrics in similar colors will be good.

Although the Materials list specifies all-cotton fabrics, you may switch to poly-blends if you have those on hand and have been thinking about a small project on which to use some of them.

The brown scallop on the edge of the ruffle is a fancy stitch on the sewing machine. Set the width for 4 or 5 mm width. If you would rather not embroider the ruffle edge, think about substituting a purchased trim.

The tiny cord is #16, but may not be easily obtainable. Use the next thicker cording or use preshrunk cotton baby knitting yarn to make a pretty narrow cord.

Before you begin working, check the Basic Sewing Supplies list on page 11 and the Basic Quilting Supplies list on page 12 to make sure you have everything you will need on hand.

Assembling the Postage Stamp Stripes

Taking care to make ¼-inch seams, sew the 1-inch squares—the stamps—into ten strips of seventeen each. Trim the seam allowances to ⅛ inch and press. (There are quick strip assembly techniques that make assemblies like

Materials

Ivory print, 100% cotton,
    42″ wide—1¼ yard

Dark brown solid, 100% cotton,
    42″ wide—⅛ yard

Dark brown and white gingham
    print, 100% cotton, 42″ wide—
    ¼ yard

Enough scraps of brown,
    eggshell, and rose prints to cut
    250 1″ squares

The smallest cotton cording
    available

Traditional polyester batting—
    17″ × 19″

#50 off-white cotton mercerized
    sewing thread for piecing and
    machine quilting

#50 dark brown cotton mercerized
    sewing thread for machine
    embroidery on ruffle edge

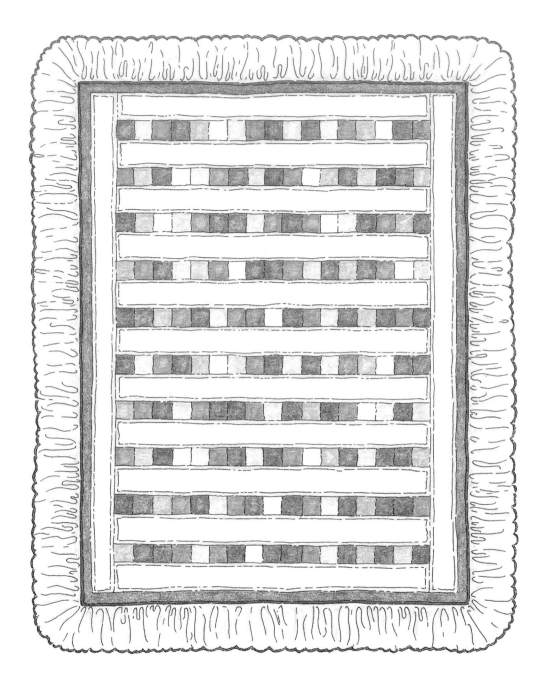

this fast and accurate, but generally the variety of combinations in the strips will be more limited. For a little project like this, I like to piece the strips individually, enjoying picking out the pieces to make a pretty pattern. If you anticipate a large project, read one of the many quick-piecing quilt project books for detailed instructions.)

Assembling the Quilt

Beginning with an ivory print strip, alternate the stamp stripes with the eleven 1½ × 13½-inch ivory strips to make one large piece. Trim the seams and press them toward the stamps.

Sew the two remaining longer ivory strips to the long sides of the piece to complete the print frame. Trim the seams and press toward the stamps.

Stitch the two longer brown strips to the two side pieces just stitched. Next stitch the remaining brown strips to the top and bottom edges to complete the brown border. Trim the seams and press toward the brown.

Stitch the bias gingham strips into one piece 2 yards long. Following the instructions for corded piping on page 22, make the piping. Trim the seam allowance of the finished cording to ¼ inch.

Matching raw edges and clipping at the corners, stitch the cording to the right side of the quilt top.

Layer the quilt back, the batting, and the top. Pin securely. Using the off-white sewing thread on both top and bobbin of the sewing machine, quilt as follows: Stitch "in the ditch" around all four sides of each postage stamp stripe. Quilt ¼ inch from the seam line on each ivory print strip. These lines are shown on the drawing of the quilt.

Join the five ruffle strips into one piece with small seams. Press ½" to the wrong side for a hem. With the brown thread, stitch a decorative scallop edge through the double thickness of the pressed hem. Place the scallop about ¼ inch from the edge. Trim away the extra fabric along the outline of the scallops. Gather the raw edge of the ruffle to fit the outside edge of the quilt.

Trim the backing and batting to match the pieced top. Trim another ¼ inch from the batting.

Pin the batting and backing out of the way. Pin the gathered ruffle to the top of the quilt. This ruffle is quite full, but it is still necessary to put as much extra fullness as possible at the corners to make the ruffle lie flat.

Stitch the ruffle to the quilt top. Unpin the backing and turn the raw edges to the inside along the seam line. Stitch in place with small hand stitches.

Quilt "in the ditch" along the brown seam line.

Cutting Guide

From the ivory print cut:
   The quilt backing, 17 × 19 inches
   5 ruffle strips 3 × 42 inches
   11 strips 1½ × 13½ inches
   2 strips 1½ × 17½ inches
From the dark brown cut:
   2 strips 1 × 17½ inches
   2 strips 1 × 16 inches
From the gingham cut:
   Enough 1½-inch bias strips to total 2 yards
From the assorted prints cut:
   250 1-inch squares (in this number include a few squares cut from the gingham and the dark brown)

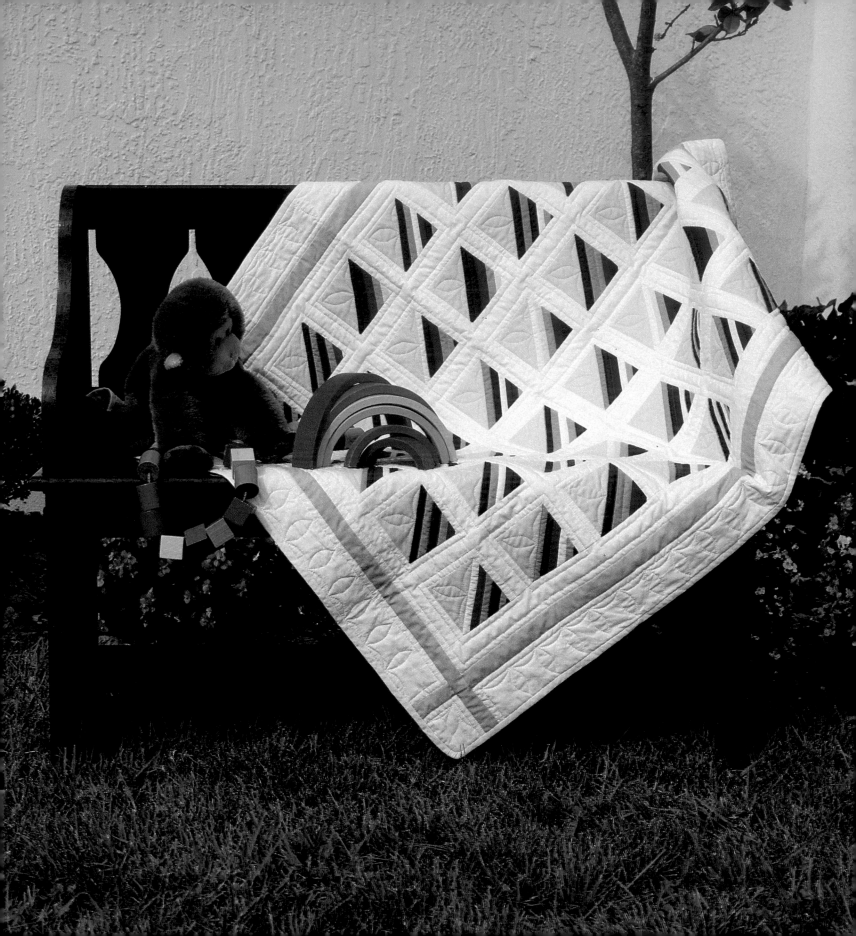

RAINBOW

A CRIB-SIZE BIT OF SUNSHINE
Finished size: 37″ × 44½″

ASBRIGHT AS A RAINBOW IN THE FIRST sunshine after a shower, this little quilt has the closely quilted, soft look of an older quilt as a result of the combination of cotton batting and machine quilting. The design is a smaller version of the old Roman Stripes pattern often favored by quilters for the many ways the blocks may be set and the variety of colors and patterns that can be used. This sparkling version in crayon colors would be a wonderful addition to the nursery for either a girl or boy. The quilt and a yellow dust ruffle edged with the rainbow striped border would be a beautiful beginning point for decorating a cheerful room.

Although this piece was quilted by machine to achieve the dimensions of an old quilt, the traditional pattern requires tying off and burying many thread ends. The finishing process is definitely worth the time, as the machine quilting is very fast and the quilt very strong.

If you prefer to quilt by hand, substitute a traditional polyester batting for the cotton. (Remember, cotton is a little more difficult to stitch than the softer polyester.) Your heirloom quilt will be smoother and wonderfully enhanced by the love put in all those stitches.

Materials
Yellow muslin, 100% cotton,
    42″ wide—3¾ yards
Four rainbow colors muslin, 100%
    cotton, 42″ wide—¼ yard or a
    fat quarter of each
Pale blue muslin, 100% cotton,
    42″ wide—½ yard
Medium blue muslin, 100%
    cotton, 42″ wide—½ yard

Finding the Materials
The cotton quilt batting contributes as much to the character of this quilt as the design and colors. It should be easy to find, but if the crib size is elusive, consider cutting down a twin to 2 inches larger than the finished size noted above.

Most quilt shops stock a wide range of these cotton muslin solids. They are sturdy and a delight to sew. The colors used in the rainbow stripes of the finished quilt are bright red, orange, yellow, dark green, medium blue, purple, and pale blue.

continued

Traditional 100% cotton quilt
   batting—crib size
Matching quilting thread—yellow
#50 off-white cotton mercerized
   thread for piecing

Cutting and Construction of the Rainbow Patches

If you have purchased ¼-yard pieces of fabric for the rainbow colors, rather than the fat quarters, cut them in half to make two pieces 9 × 22 inches. Cut the four rainbow colors into strips ⅞ × 22 inches. Also cut several strips this size of the remaining pale blue and medium blue, and of the yellow fat quarter. These will all be used to make rainbow patches.

After checking carefully to ascertain that the seam allowance is a scant ¼ inch and using the off-white thread for construction, stitch six assorted ⅞ × 22-inch strips into a rainbow-striped rectangle 22 inches long, as shown in Figure 1. Alternate the sequence of the colors so each unit is different.

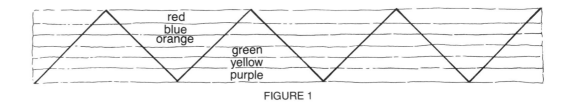

red
blue
orange
green
yellow
purple

FIGURE 1

Cutting Guide

If you have purchased ¼-yard
   pieces of fabric for the rainbow
   colors, rather than the fat
   quarters, cut them in half to
   make two pieces 9 × 22 inches.
From the yellow cut:
   The quilt backing, 39 × 46½
   inches
   A fat quarter to use as a
   rainbow color
   40 pieces 2⅛ × 2⅞ inches
   9 pieces 2⅛ × 28¼ inches
   2 strips 2⅛ × 39 inches
   2 strips 3 × 39 inches
   2 strips 3 × 31 inches
   4 corner blocks 3 × 3 inches
From the medium blue cut:
   2 border strips 1½ × 38½
   inches
   2 border strips 1½ × 39 inches
   4 strips 1½ × 3 inches
From the pale blue cut:
   4 strips 2⅞ × 42 inches

The striped rectangle should be 2⅞ inches wide and look like Figure 1. (Note that the widths of the two outside pieces in the drawing are wider, as the seam allowances on one side have not been stitched.) Trim the seam allowances to ⅛ inch and press. Because the seam allowance is so critical, I suggest that one unit be made, then the template (Figure 2) cut and placed on the block and checked to make sure it is the correct width. The template should fit on the

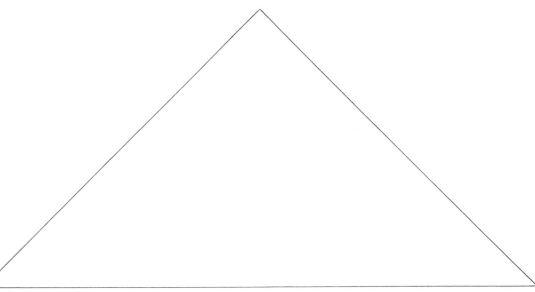

FIGURE 2

block as shown by the heavier line in Figure 1. If the block is too wide, increase the seam allowance slightly; if too small, make the allowance smaller. There is plenty of fabric to make an extra block if necessary.

Place the template on the block as shown in Figure 1 and cut six striped triangles from each block. Repeat to cut forty-eight rainbow-striped triangles.

Cut the pale blue 2⅞-inch strips into forty-eight triangles, using the template as for the rainbow stripes.

Construction of the Rainbow Squares

With right sides together, stitch the long side of one striped triangle to the long side of one pale blue triangle to make a square. Trim the seam allowance to ⅛ inch and press toward the stripes. Repeat to make forty-eight rainbow patches.

Assembling the Quilt Top

Arrange the rainbow patches in eight rows of six squares each, distributing the different color sequences evenly throughout. Place the patches so the pale blue "sky" triangle is always at the top, as illustrated on the drawing of the quilt.

Join the patches into rows by stitching the forty yellow 2⅛ × 2⅞-inch rectangles between them. Begin and end each row with a rainbow patch. Trim seams and press toward the pieced blocks.

Join the rainbow block rows with the nine 2⅛-inch yellow strips, beginning and ending with yellow. Trim the seams and press them toward the yellow.

Stitch the two 2⅛ × 39-inch yellow pieces to the long sides of the panel, completing the yellow frame. Trim the seams and press.

Blue Borders

Stitch two 1½ × 38½ inch medium blue strips to the yellow just attached. Cut off and discard any small excess at the ends. Trim the seams and press the allowances toward the blue.

Stitch one of the 3 × 39-inch yellow strips to the blue on each side to complete the side borders. Trim the seam allowances and press toward the blue.

Stitch the other 1½-inch-wide medium blue strips to the top and bottom edges of the piece. Trim seam allowances and press toward the blue.

Outside Border

Stitch together in this order: (1) a yellow corner block, (2) a 1½ × 3-inch medium blue piece, (3) one of the remaining long yellow border pieces, (4) another medium blue 1½ × 3 inch piece, and (5) another corner block. (Before attaching the second blue piece, measure against the top or bottom edge of the pieced quilt to make sure the lines of the blue will match the vertical blue side borders. Adjust if necessary.) Repeat for the other end of the quilt.

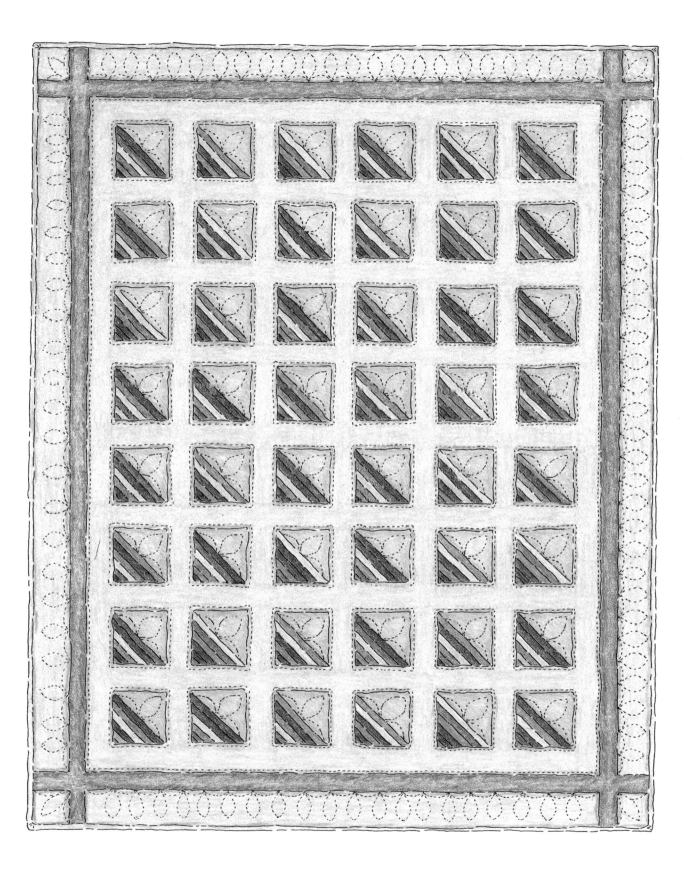

Assembling the Quilt

Press the top well. Place the quilt back on a flat surface wrong side up. Place batting on top; follow with the pieced quilt top right side up. Pin securely. Baste the layers together.

Make a template from Quilting Design 1 for the Rainbow Patch on lightweight paper. Trace the entire drawing as it is shown, then cut it out. To trace the quilting design, match the edges of the shaded yellow area to the rainbow portion of the block. Trace just the dotted quilting lines onto the blue triangle.

Quilt "in the ditch" around the rainbow patches and also ¼ inch outside each patch. Quilt also on the inside of the blue borders as shown by the tiny dots on the color drawing of the quilt. Quilt also "in the ditch" between all the rainbow stripes. Finish the petal designs on all the blue triangles.

Smooth the edges and trim all three layers evenly. Baste them together. From the remaining yellow fabric cut 1-inch bias strips to reach around the outside edges of the quilt. Following the bias binding instructions on page 23, bind the edges of the quilt to finish it.

Trace Quilting Design 2 for a template for the four yellow corner blocks. Cut out the template and match the straight edges to the seam lines. Trace the quilting line shown by the short slashed lines.

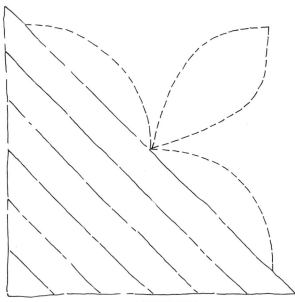

QUILTING DESIGN 1
Quilting Design for the Rainbow Patches
Quilt on dashed lines.

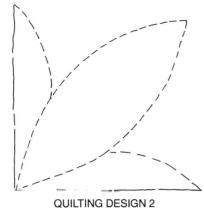

QUILTING DESIGN 2
Quilting Design for the Four Corner Blocks
Match the straight edges to the seams and quilt on the dashed lines.

Using the same procedure, trace Quilting Design 3 for the borders and place the designs as shown on the drawing of the quilt. Begin marking at the center and work to the ends, placing the straight line on the seam line to assure correct alignment. (Since this template will be quite fragile, you will want to allow the paper to extend an inch or so beyond the seam line.)

Quilt on the lines to finish your little Rainbow!

QUILTING DESIGN 3
Quilting Design for the Outer Borders
Match the straight edge to the seam and quilt on the dashed lines.

LITTLE PRINCESS

RUFFLES AND HEARTS FOR DOLLY
Finished size: 15″ × 20½″ exclusive of 3″ ruffle

Iᴛ'S HARD TO DECIDE IF IT IS THE BEAU-
tiful materials or the delicate pink stenciled hearts that make this doll quilt so appealing.
Combined they make a gift any little girl would cherish. An added bonus for the maker is that
the quilt can be made very quickly.

If you are considering making a crib-size quilt, this design has good ideas and would be
very easy to enlarge. Either enlarge the heart stencil design and the size of the blocks or
multiply the number of small blocks to make a standard crib size. This will make a very
feminine and delicate quilt.

Materials

White broadcloth or fine muslin,
　42″ wide—½ yard
Swiss eyelet edging, 3½″ wide,
　white—6 yards
Swiss eyelet beading, ½″ wide,
　white—2¼ yards
Double-faced satin ribbon,
　¼″ wide, pink—4½ yards
Low-loft polyester batting—
　approximately 20″ × 25″
#50 white cotton mercerized
　thread for quilting
Stencil crayon—baby pink
Stencil film—4″ × 4″
Washout pen

Finding the Materials

Any pretty white opaque fabric will make a lovely quilt. The stenciling will
be prettier if the weave is fairly even and as fine as good-quality muslin.
The lovely Swiss eyelet can be found in a smocking or fine fabrics store. If not
available in your area, substitute any pretty eyelet or make a self-ruffle with a
lace edge.

Before shopping for materials, check the Basic Sewing Supplies list on page
11 and the Stenciling Supplies list on page 26 to make sure you have everything
you will need on hand.

Cutting Guide

Matching the selvage edges, fold the fabric in half and cut into two pieces
18 × 21 inches. Set one piece aside for the quilt back.

With a washout pen, divide the other piece into quarters by placing one
horizontal and one vertical line through the center, shown as lines A and B on
the Layout Drawing. Measure out from the two lines and mark a 3-inch grid as
shown on the drawing. After the grid has been marked, notice that the borders
on the long sides are a bit wider than those on the top and bottom of the piece.
Trim the wider ones to match the others.

FIGURE 1

Stenciling

Trace the heart stencil drawing (Figure 1) onto film and cut it out. (Be sure to remove any traces of ink from the edges of the film.) Using the stencil crayon, place a heart in the center of each square on the marked quilt top. Work the paint into the edges of the heart more heavily to achieve the shaded look evident in the stenciled heart shown here.

Assembly

Insert the ribbon into the beading before stitching it to the quilt top. Save the surplus for the bows at top and bottom.

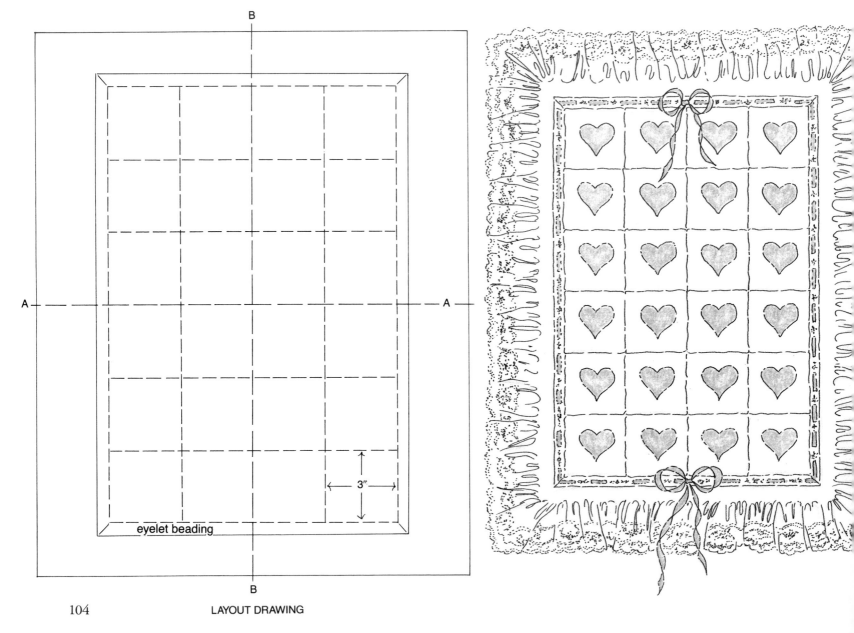

B

A — A

3"

eyelet beading

B

LAYOUT DRAWING

Mitering the corners, stitch the beading to the quilt top outside the drawn grid as shown on the Layout Drawing.

Layer the quilt back, the batting, and the stenciled top. Pin and baste well. Quilt on all the blue lines shown on the Quilting Guide. Also quilt around the hearts, placing the stitching on the background fabric at the edge of the hearts.

Gather the eyelet edging and sew it to the outside edge of the quilt top, holding the batting and backing out of the way. Allow extra fullness at the corners so the ruffle will lie flat.

Trim the batting to ¼ inch smaller than the quilt top. Turn the raw edge of the backing to the inside and stitch the backing to the top with invisible stitches.

Make bows with the remainder of the ribbon and attach them as shown on the drawing.

The Quilting Guide shows one complete square at the corner of the quilt. Notice the way the eyelet beading has been mitered to turn the corner. Quilt around the pink edges of the hearts and on all the blue lines except those that indicate the ruffle.

PATCHED HEARTS

AN ENDEARING PINK CHARMER FOR THE CRIB
Finished size: 40″ × 50″

THE HEART, WHICH HAS ALWAYS BEEN prominent in quilt design, is not only a delightful expression of love, joy, and home, it is also a very versatile motif. Its simple outline can convey messages of many meanings, all of them cheerful and loving. For this bright little quilt, the heart is wide and comfortable, reminiscent of the folk art found in Pennsylvania. The easy patchwork in four small prints contributes to a country feeling that could be the beginning of a wonderful little girl's room.

The patchwork for the hearts is made very simply by sewing together strips of the four prints, then using a template to trace and cut out twenty hearts. The hearts were then machine-appliquéd to the 8-inch white muslin squares.

Joining the squares with lattice strips and blocks of two prints in the patchwork carries the pink color to the edges, where a striped border of the prints, narrow bias binding, and pink calico backing finish this pretty quilt.

Finding the Materials

Choose four related small prints for the prettiest hearts. For the pictured quilt, the prints include one (#1) that is a pink background with very small white hearts; another (#2) has a pink ground with a fine fernlike all-over design. The third pink print (#3) is a sweet calico that brings in a touch of blue in some of the little flowers, while a white background calico (#4) features tiny rose sprays.

Before you begin working, check the Basic Sewing Supplies list on page 11 and the Basic Quilting Supplies list on page 12 to make sure you have everything you will need on hand.

Materials

White muslin, 100% cotton, 42″ wide—1 yard
Pink print (#1), 100% cotton, 42″ wide—⅜ yard
Pink print (#2), 100% cotton, 42″ wide—⅜ yard
Pink print (#3), 100% cotton, 42″ wide—2¼ yards
White print (#4), 100% cotton, 42″ wide—⅝ yard
Cotton quilt batting—crib size
#50 white cotton mercerized thread for quilting and construction
#50 pink cotton mercerized thread for decorative appliqué stitching
Stencil film—8″ × 8″
Washout pen or #2 pencil

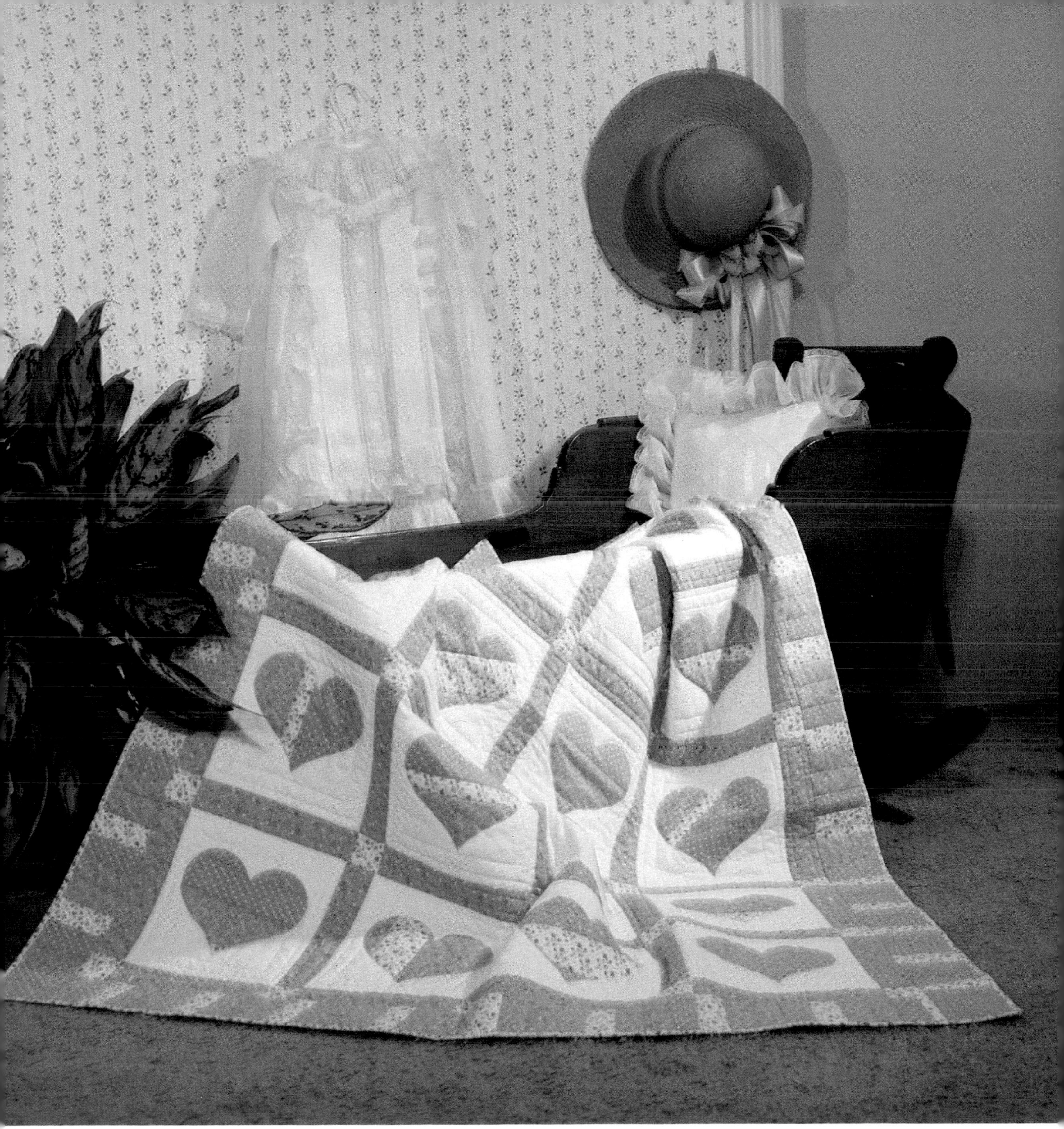

HEART TEMPLATE

Cutting Guide

From the white muslin cut:
   20 squares 8 × 8 inches
From pink print #1 cut:
   1 strip 2½ × 42 inches (A)
   1 strip 3½ × 42 inches (B)
   4 corner blocks 3¼ × 3¼ inches
From pink print #2 cut:
   1 strip 2¾ × 42 inches (A)
   1 strip 3 × 42 inches (B)
From pink print #3 cut:
   The quilt backing, 41 × 51
   inches
   1 strip 2¾ × 42 inches (A)
   1 strip 3 × 42 inches (B)
   49 lattice strips 2 × 8 inches
From white print #4 cut:
   1 strip 2½ × 42 inches (A)
   1 strip 1 × 42 inches (B)
   30 lattice blocks 2 × 2 inches
   Enough 1½-inch bias strips to
   make 190 inches

Constructing the Heart Blocks

Stitch together the 42-inch lengths of the four prints noted as (A) in the Cutting Guide list, beginning with print #1 and continuing in numerical sequence. Trim the seams to ⅛ inch and press. The piece made should measure 9½ × 42 inches.

Make similar strip using the strips marked (B) in the Cutting Guide. Change the print sequence for this piece. Trim the seams and press.

Cut a template of clear plastic using the Heart Template (*above*) as a pattern.

Using a washout pen or a #2 pencil, trace twenty hearts on the pieced strips. Turn the template often so some are cut with the stripes horizontal, some with the stripes vertical, and many with the stripes at different slanted angles. There should also be several that are made up of only three of the prints. The clear plastic template will allow you to move it to many pleasing positions, and the quilt is prettier if a variety of different angles is used. Do *not* cut out the hearts.

Set the sewing machine for a moderately short straight stitch—about 1½ mm length or 8 stitches to the inch. With pink thread, stitch around each heart, placing the stitching on the traced lines.

Cut out the hearts, cutting just outside the stitching to avoid cutting the thread.

Center the hearts on the 8-inch white muslin squares. Pin in place. Using pink thread and a zigzag stitch, appliqué the hearts, placing the stitching so that the stitches cover the raw edges of the hearts. Press.

Assembling the Quilt Top

Lay the heart squares on a flat surface in five rows of four each. Arrange the assortment of patterns in the most pleasing way, or look at the color drawing of the quilt as a guide for this placement. It is exactly like the pictured quilt.

Beginning and ending with a 2 × 8-inch lattice strip, stitch the squares into five rows. Each row should contain four appliquéd heart squares and six lattice strips. Trim the seams and press.

Beginning and ending with a white print 2-inch lattice block, stitch four 8-inch lattice strips and five white blocks into a strip. Make six strips.

Join the five rows of heart blocks with the strips just constructed. Begin and end with a narrow lattice strip. Check carefully to make certain the seams match exactly. Trim the seams and press. The pieced field measures 36¾ × 45¾ inches.

Striped Border

Cut from each of the prints four strips measuring 1¾ × 42 inches. Stitch the strips together in a striped pattern, alternating the prints in a regular sequence. Trim the seams and press.

Cutting across the seams, cut the pieced strips into 3¼-inch pieces as illustrated in Figure 1. Stitch enough together side by side to make a border piece 45¾ × 3¼ inches. Repeat to make another strip the same size and two more measuring 36¾ × 3¼ inches.

Stitch the first two borders to the long sides of the pieced field. Trim the seams and press.

Stitch a corner block to the end of each of the remaining border pieces. Stitch these borders to the top and bottom of the field.

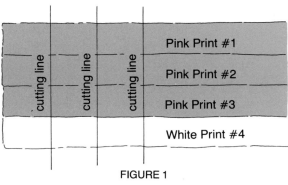

FIGURE 1

Piecing the Striped Border

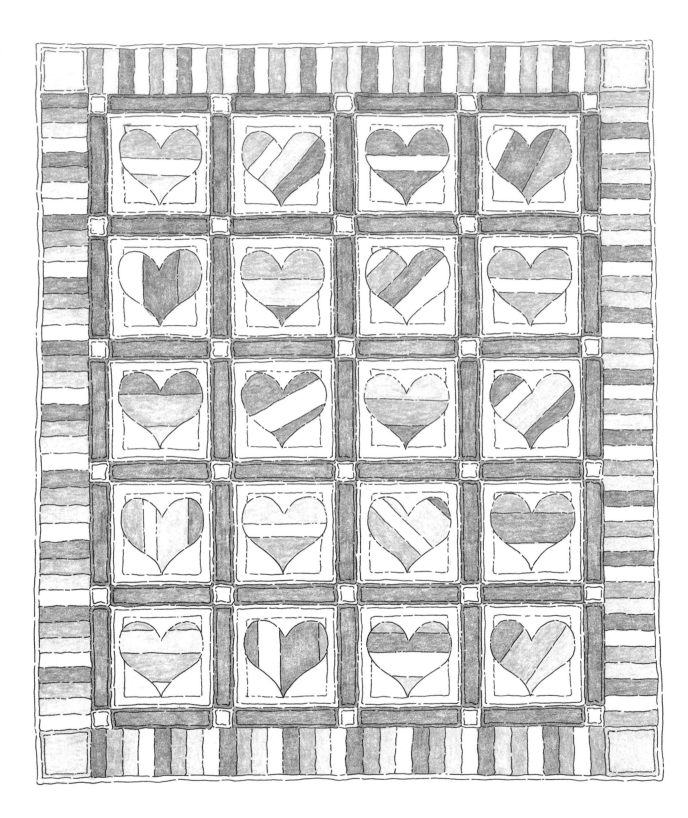

Assembling and Quilting

Layer the quilt backing, the batting, and the top. Smooth out all wrinkles and pin the layers together with safety pins in preparation for machine quilting.

The Quilting Guide shows one corner of the quilt as an aid for the quilting placement. For maximum beauty, quilt each line shown on the drawing except the two outside edge lines, which depict the bias binding. This means many thread ends to tie, but the cotton batting really should be heavily quilted, and the tying is really much faster than hand quilting.

Begin by stitching "in the ditch" around the squares to stabilize the layers. Remove the pins. Then complete the decorative stitching in the lattice strips and squares.

For the heart squares, you will want to quilt on the piecing lines of the hearts and around the edges of the hearts, placing the stitches on the background fabric just outside the pink zigzag stitching. Then stitch a line around the square ¼ inch in from the seam line and the broken line—the heart overlaps it—½ inch in from the first line.

Finally, stitch the borders, placing the stitching "in the ditch" as in the rest of the quilting.

When all quilting has been completed, finish the edges with bias binding from print #4, following the instructions on page 23.

QUILTING GUIDE
Stitch on all lines except the outside two which denote the bias binding.

LITTLE LAMBS

A LITTLE PIECE OF STENCILING MAGIC FOR THE NURSERY

Finished size: 41″ × 48″ exclusive of the 3″ ruffle

HIS LITTLE QUILT IS CERTAIN TO BE A favorite with both baby and mother. It is soft and fluffy to make a warm bed, while the dear little lambs add just the right touch of whimsy. The blue ribbons could easily be changed to any color to fit a special nursery. In addition to their use on the quilt, the stencil designs are appropriate for pillows, curtains, and walls for a coordinated look.

Materials

White 100% cotton, 42″ wide—
    8 yards
Traditional quilt batting—crib size
#50 white cotton mercerized
    thread for quilting and
    construction
Cotton cord—5⅛ yards
Stencil crayons or paint—blue,
    gray, black, pink, and green
Stencil film, 9″ × 12″—6 pieces
Fine-point fabric markers—black,
    pink, yellow, and green
Washout pen

For the Optional Ruffle and Blue
    Cording:
An additional 2 yards of the white
    cotton
Blue 100% cotton, 42″ wide, to
    match stencil blue—½ yard

Finding the Materials

Choose a smooth white cotton so the stencils will create nice sharp outlines. If you switch to a poly-blend fabric, check your paint labels to make certain the colors will be fast on that combination of fibers.

The pictured quilt was colored with stencil crayons, because they make it so easy to shade colors more heavily along the edges of the film. The flowers and grass at the lambs' feet were traced with the fabric markers. Try to match the pink and green to the stencil crayons. Look for pretty baby colors in both crayons and markers, and use them lightly for a delicate look.

The drawing of the quilt shows it with a white cording finish, while the finished quilt in the photograph suggests an optional blue cording and a 3-inch white ruffle. The ruffle is double—the fabric cut 7 inches wide and folded in half before gathering. The blue cord is inserted in the seam as a fine tailoring touch. Because you have two finishing options, the extra ruffle fabric and the yardage for the blue cord are listed as optional in the Materials list.

Before you begin working, check the Basic Sewing Supplies list on page 11, the Basic Quilting Supplies list on page 12, and the Stenciling Supplies list on page 26 to make sure you have everything you will need on hand.

Cutting Guide

From the white cotton cut:
  The quilt top and backing, each
  42 × 49 inches
  Bias strips 1½ inches wide to
  total 5⅛ yards
If optional ruffle is being
  made, cut:
  12 strips 7 inches wide
  across the full width of the
  white fabric
If optional blue cording is being
  made, cut:
  Bias strips 1½ inches wide to
  total 5⅛ yards (eliminate the
  white bias strips)

Marking and Stenciling

Cut a 9 × 9-inch square from stencil film. Draw a 7 × 7-inch square inside the square of film, centering it carefully so the stencil will be an accurate measuring guide. Cut a little hole at each corner of the 7-inch square—just large enough for the point of a washout pen. Use this stencil film template to mark the divisions for the design on the quilt top. (This method will avoid making marks that have to be removed before painting.)

Lay the quilt top flat on a flat protected working space. Measure down from one end of the piece 4 inches and in 4 inches from the selvage, and place one of the top openings of the template at that point, making certain the other corners are straight and on grain. Mark a dot through the holes at the corners of the 7-inch square. Move the square template, placing two holes over two of the markings just made and mark two more corners through the other holes. Continue moving the template to mark six rows of five squares each. The piece should look like Figure 1.

FIGURE 1

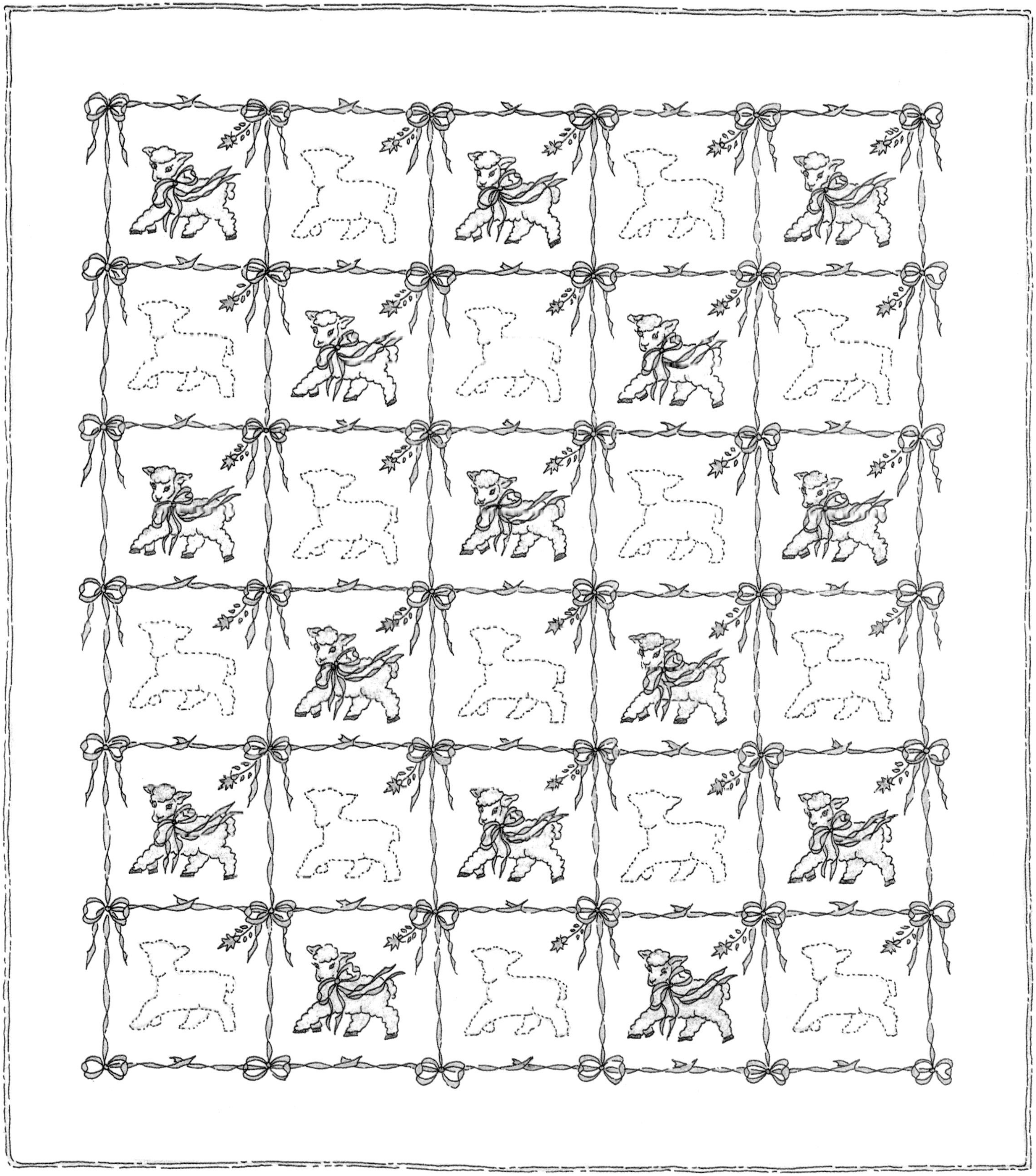

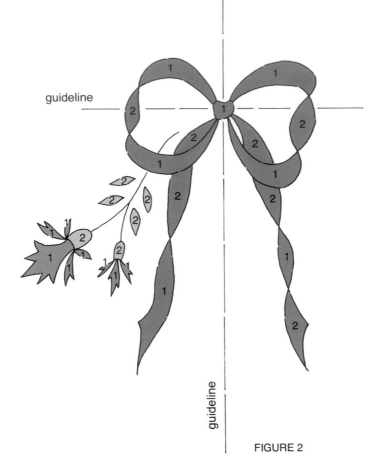

guideline

guideline

FIGURE 2

The Blue Ribbons

Cut two pieces of stencil film 5 × 9 inches. On one—this will be Stencil 1—trace the areas of the bow and the flowers numbered 1 on Figure 2. Place the knot of the bow about 1½ inches from the top end of the stencil film. Trace also the horizontal and vertical guidelines, extending the vertical line to the bottom edge of the film. On the other—Stencil 2—trace the areas of the bow and the leaves numbered 2 and both guidelines as before. Cut out all but the guidelines.

Beginning with Stencil 1, paint a bow and flowers at the corners of each square marked on the quilt top. Place the stencil with the opening for the knot centered over the dot and the vertical line extending so it intersects the dot below. Paint the bow blue, the flowers pink. You can prevent accidentally smearing blue paint into the openings for the flowers by putting a little piece of tape temporarily over those openings.

On the left side of the quilt the flower sprays will extend into the border. To keep the border plain to match the other three sides, *do not paint the sprays on this side.*

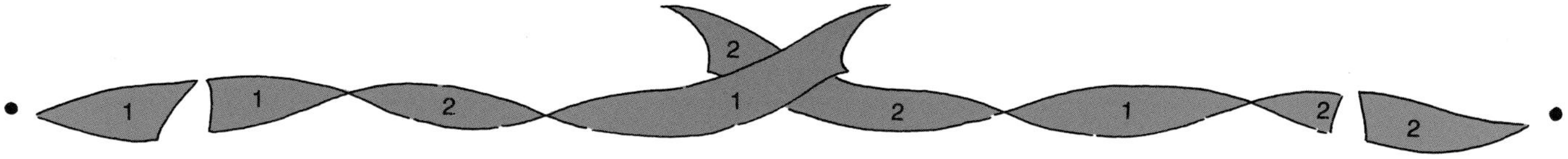

FIGURE 3

Place Stencil 2 in the same manner and, using the same blue paint or stencil crayon, color the portions of the bow on that stencil. Color the leaves green. Repeat for all corners. *Notice that on the row at the bottom of the quilt, the two trailing ribbon ends under the bows have been omitted.*

Cut two pieces of stencil film 3 × 9 inches. On one—Stencil 3—trace and cut the areas of the ribbon on Figure 3 that are numbered 1. On the other—Stencil 4—trace and cut the areas numbered 2. On both stencils copy the dot at each end. Use these stencils for the horizontal ribbons of all the squares.

Using the blue ribbon color, paint the horizontals. When you place the stencils, position the dots over the centers of the knots where the first markings were made.

Cut two pieces of stencil film 3 × 9 inches. On one—Stencil 5—trace and cut the ribbon areas of Figure 4 marked 1. On the other—Stencil 6—trace and cut out the areas marked 2. As before, trace the centering dots also. These two stencils are for all the vertical ribbons. Place the dots as you did with the horizontal ribbons, and color the vertical sides of all the blocks.

Since these pairs of stencils line up to make continuous lines, it is best to trace and cut as carefully as possible. However, if you look at the color drawing showing one block, you will see that there are little areas where the twisted blue ribbon sections do not meet precisely. These combined with the subtle shading of the crayon add a hand-painted dimension when the quilting lines are added. The quilting lines will not be as deep as the black outlines on the color drawing, but they have a similar outlining effect.

The Stenciled Lambs

Before beginning to place the stenciled lambs, note that they are on alternating squares. The unpainted quilted lambs decorate the plain squares.

On a 9 × 9-inch piece of film, trace and cut out the parts of the lamb numbered 1 on Figure 5 to make Stencil 7. Trace a portion of the horizontal ribbon below the lamb on Figure 5 to use as a guide for placing the lamb in the squares. Applying the paint sparingly, color this portion of the lamb gray. Work the paint more heavily in the edges of the stencil, but leave the body a very pale color.

On another 9 × 9-inch piece of stencil film, trace and cut out the areas of Figure 5 labeled 2—this will be Stencil 8. Paint the bow and ribbons blue. Again, place a piece of tape over the opening for the face if the blue color is

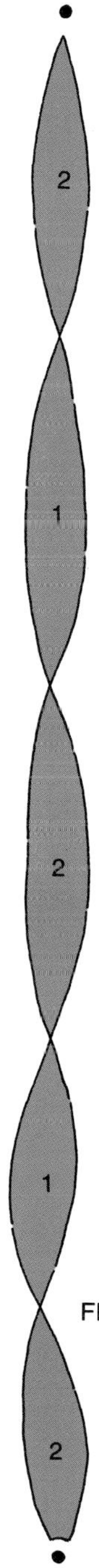

FIGURE 4

117

liable to be carried into that area. Using the black crayon, but being sparing to create a deeper shade of gray rather than a dense black, color the face, hooves, and parts of ears on that stencil. Use the color drawing as guide for this coloring.

On a third 9 × 9-inch piece of stencil film, trace and cut out the areas marked 3 on Figure 5—to make Stencil 9. Color the head, tail, and legs gray, the eyes and the balance of the bow and ribbons blue.

Make a tracing of the lamb's eyes, mouth, hooves, the flowers, grass, and the horizontal ribbon on Figure 5. Make the lines heavy enough to be visible through the fabric of the quilt top. Place the tracing under the fabric, using the hooves and ribbon as guides, and draw in the flowers and grass, using the pink, yellow, and green fabric markers. Use the black pen to outline the eyes and mouth. At the same time, draw the green stems of the flower sprays beside the bows.

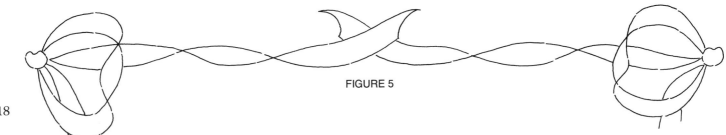

FIGURE 5

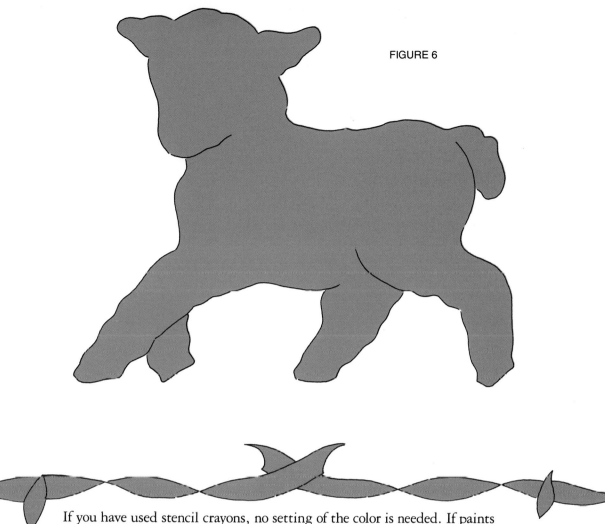

FIGURE 6

If you have used stencil crayons, no setting of the color is needed. If paints were used, fix the color now using the manufacturer's instructions.

The Quilted Lambs

Make a tracing of Figure 6, including the ribbon at the bottom. Place this under the fabric, and using a washout pen and the ribbon as a guide for placement, trace the lambs in the remaining squares.

Assembly and Quilting

Layer the quilt back, the batting, and the stenciled top, smoothing out all wrinkles. Pin the three together and then baste them, placing the rows of stitches about 2 inches apart in horizontal rows.

Using the #50 white cotton thread, hand-quilt around all areas of color except the flowers and grass. Quilt also the outline of the unpainted lambs in the alternate squares.

When all the quilting has been completed, dab the lines of the washout pen to remove the blue outlines of the quilted unpainted lambs from those squares. Allow the top to dry. If some of the blue comes back, wet it again.

Finishing

Trim all four sides to the same border width. For a tailored quilt with the white corded piping, make the piping following the instructions on page 22. Holding the backing and the batting out of the way, stitch it to the outside edges of the quilt, turn the raw edges to the inside, and whipstitch them closed with small invisible stitches.

For a quilt with piping and a gathered double ruffle, make the blue piping and stitch it to the outside edges of the quilt top, holding the batting and backing out of the way. Stitch the 7-inch-wide ruffle pieces together to make one continuous piece. Fold it in half so it is 3½ inches wide, press in the fold, and pin the raw edges together.

With the machine, stitch two rows of gathering stitches, placing the first ¼ inch from the raw edge, the second ¼ inch from the first. Pull up the bobbin threads to gather the piece to fit the outside edge of the quilt.

Pin the ruffle to the quilt top, matching the raw edges of the piping, the quilt top, and the ruffle. Stitch. Turn the raw edges to the inside and whipstitch them together with small invisible stitches.

LITTLE STARS

A ONE-PIECE DOLL COUNTERPANE
Finished size: 19″ × 26″

THE ONE-PIECE QUILT, OR COUNTER-pane, was most often the treasured "best" bed covering, usually heavily quilted and, because it was carefully stored as a rule, the one most likely to survive the years. Few doll quilts were made in this idiom, but those that were seem to have been made as part of a wardrobe for a very special doll. This little version could well fall into that category. Its silky feel and pretty quilting pattern make it a project that will be fun for a quilt-loving adult to make and for a lucky little girl to treasure.

Materials

Pastel blue Swiss batiste, 100% cotton, 42″ wide—21″ × 28″
White Swiss batiste, 100% cotton, 42″ wide—21″ × 28″
Washout pen
Low-loft polyester quilt batting— 21″ × 28″
#50 white cotton mercerized thread for quilting and construction
White crocheted edging— 2½ yards
Masking tape—¼″ wide

Finding the Materials

The Swiss batiste adds a silky softness to this elegant little quilt, but as for most projects, another batiste may be substituted with beautiful results. Just be certain to choose a soft fabric woven tightly enough to prevent migration of fibers from the batting.

Although the pictured quilt is made with one blue and one white side, if both sides were the same, 28 inches of 42-inch-wide fabric would be sufficient.

Look for a narrow edging—not necessarily crocheted—heavy enough to add a pretty edge to the quilt. Tatting, if available, is beautiful. Another possibility is an edging of the heavier Cluny variety.

Before you begin working, check the Basic Sewing Supplies list on page 11 and the Basic Quilting Supplies list on page 12 to make sure you have everything you will need on hand.

Cutting and Marking Guide

After the batiste has been washed and pressed, cut one blue and one white piece 21 × 28 inches. Mark one for the top as follows:

Trace the double star design—Figure 1—onto a piece of paper and cut it out. Trace the 5-inch square around the star and cut it out to use as a template.

Using a washout pen, draw an 18 × 25-inch rectangle on the batiste. Mark the center lines A and B as shown on the Layout Drawing.

Place the square template on the batiste with the center on line B and the edge 1 inch from line A as shown on the Layout Drawing. Trace around the template with the washout pen. Place a second square on the other side of the center in exactly the same manner.

Leaving a 2-inch space between the bottoms of the first squares and the tops of the next ones, trace two squares below the first two, lining up the sides 1 inch from the center line as before. Repeat to trace two squares above the first two squares.

Check the measurements to be certain that the space between the squares is 2 inches. The four borders are 3 inches wide.

Measure out from the original rectangle ½ inch and mark another rectangle. This line is the seam line. There is ½-inch seam allowance beyond that.

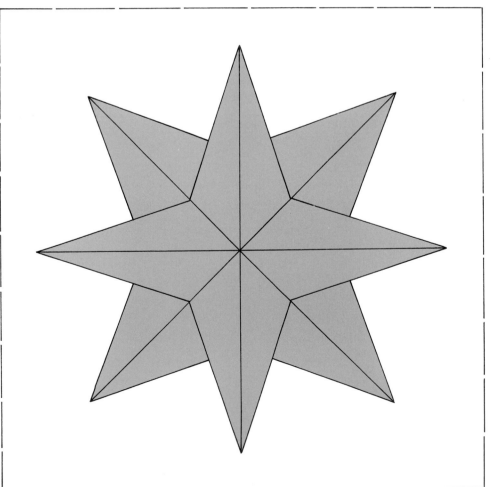

FIGURE 1

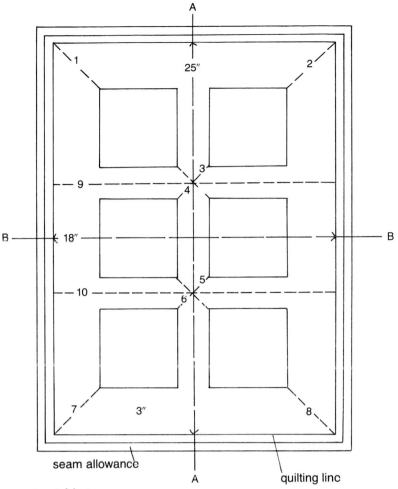

seam allowance

quilting line

LAYOUT DRAWING

Center the star template in each of the six squares and trace it. Add the straight lines inside the stars with a ruler, using Figure 1 as a guide.

The only other quilting lines you need draw are those numbered 1 through 10. Lines 1 through 8 establish the diagonals for the background pattern. Lines 9 and 10 mark the centers of the spaces where the lines turn to create the herringbone pattern.

Quilting

Quilt on each line in Figure 1, including the outline of the square. Quilt also ¼ inch inside each square.

Begin quilting the background on one of the diagonal lines. Quilt first on the line, then place a piece of masking tape along the line and stitch beside the tape. Repeat to complete the background pattern. Use the drawing of the quilt as a guide for this part of the pattern.

Complete all quilting. Trim the batting to ¼ inch shorter than the back and top. Turn the raw edges to the inside on the seam line and whipstitch them together. Quilt ½ inch from the finished edge.

By hand, whipstitch the lace edging to the outside of the quilt.

125

PETITE BÉBÉ

AN HEIRLOOM DOLL QUILT WITH SHADOW EMBROIDERY
Finished size: 18″ × 25″ exclusive of the lace edging

Lavished with a border of sprightly blue bows and trimmed with shadow embroidery, this is indeed a very special doll quilt. The silky white batiste, scalloped edges, gathered lace ruffle, flowing ribbons, and elegant script combine to make a delicate-looking little quilt that can be enjoyed and played with, then treasured for many years.

Shadow embroidery is an elegant touch which in itself is lovely, but the additional shading the overdyed floss lends to the work adds a paintlike dimension. Quilting along the edges of the embroidery puffs the bows forward to give the quilt an extra softness you will enjoy.

Finding the Materials
The beautiful batiste used for both this doll quilt and Bébé, the crib-size version following, is the fine-quality Swiss cotton used traditionally for fine hand sewing and machine "heirloom" sewing. Although it is not commonly used for quilts, it is very strong and durable. You can probably find it in a shop specializing in supplies for heirloom sewing and smocking.

The design requires that the embroidered top of the quilt be backed with a second piece of batiste. Facing the top with this extra piece of batiste emphasizes the embroidery, as the facing lies closer to the back of it than the batting would, making a prettier display of the embroidery. This piece is included in the 1½ yards of batiste on the Materials list. You could substitute a less expensive domestic batiste for the facing, thus decreasing the required Swiss batiste yardage to ¾ yard.

Materials
White Swiss batiste, 100% cotton, 42″ wide—1½ yards
Low-loft quilt batting—19″ × 26″
Six-strand overdyed cotton embroidery floss—1 skein blue; 1 yard each pink, yellow, and green
#50 white cotton mercerized thread for quilting and construction
Lace edging, cotton, 1¼″ wide—6 yards

Cutting Guide

Cut from the white batiste:
  4 pieces 21 × 27 inches
  (One is surplus.)

If it is impossible to find the Swiss batiste, use either a cotton-polyester blend batiste or a domestic batiste. Your quilt will still be an heirloom.

The lace used is an English cotton. The smocking shop again is the best place to find these beautiful laces. The discussion of lace in the Fabrics section (page 7) details the differences in laces to help you in selecting among them.

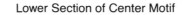

Lower Section of Center Motif

The pictured doll quilt has been embroidered with overdyed six-strand cotton floss. Refering to the Materials section again, read the caution about colorfastness, and note that this thread is packed in 20-yard skeins instead of the familiar 8 yards. If this thread is not available in your area, the quilt can be completed with one skein (8 yards) of traditional six-strand embroidery floss in medium blue. Only about a yard of pink, yellow, and green are needed.

Before you begin working, check the Basic Sewing Supplies list on page 11 and the Basic Quilting Supplies list on page 12 to make sure you have everything you will need on hand.

Marking

Use the quilt drawing for Bébé on page 134 as a reference for marking the designs onto the batiste. Petite Bébé is finished with gathered lace edging and Bébé is enlarged and has shadow quilting instead of embroidery, but the two quilts are identical in layout.

Fold one of the pieces of batiste into quarters by bringing the long sides together, then folding so the short edges meet. Press in the folds.

Trace the bow and scallop border design on paper. Include on the drawing

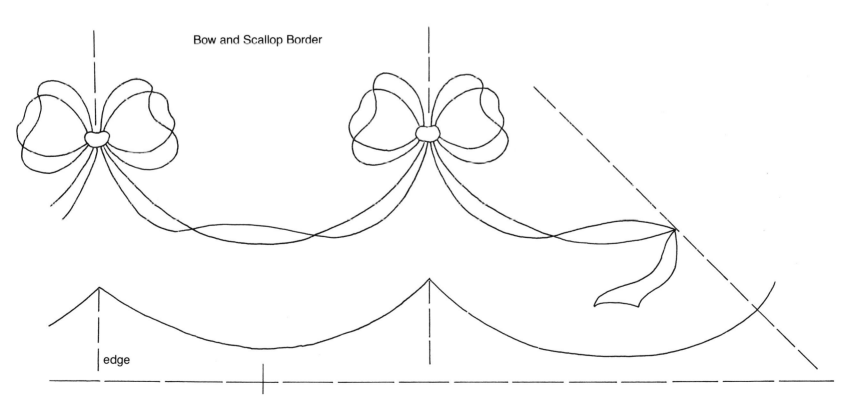

Bow and Scallop Border

edge

Upper Section of Center Motif

the dashed line marked "edge," the center mark, the dashed lines indicating the ends of a scallop, and the diagonal corner line.

With the batiste opened out flat, lay the tracing under the batiste with the edge line about ¾ inch from the edge and the center mark on one of the fold lines, then begin to trace the border. On the short sides of the piece, repeat the scallops four times, beginning and ending with the corner scallop. On the long sides repeat the scallops six times, finishing again with the corner scallop.

On a large piece of paper, trace the two sections of the center motif. Copy the dashed center lines and join the sections of design where they overlap.

Center the motif by matching the dashed lines to the fold lines of the batiste. Trace the design onto the batiste.

The Embroidery

Following the stitch instructions for shadow embroidery on page 24, work the entire design in the double herringbone stitch. Use a single strand of embroidery floss and a #7 crewel needle. All ribbons should be blue; the flower centers yellow, the flowers pink, and the leaves green.

With the sewing machine and a short straight stitch—about eight stitches to the inch on older machines, about 1½ mm on newer models—stitch exactly on the line of the scallops along the outside edge. Wash the piece to remove any markings. Roll the freshly washed piece in a towel, pressing out excess water. Place a towel on the ironing board and iron the piece dry. Work only on the wrong side to preserve the depth of the embroidery.

Finishing

On a flat surface, layer the quilt backing, the batting, the facing, and the quilt top. Begin by laying out the quilt back wrong side up and smoothing out any wrinkles. Place the batting on top of the backing. Follow with the facing and finish with the quilt top, right side up. Pin the layers together, then baste them together.

Quilt around all the embroidery, placing the stitches along the edge of the stitches on the surface. Quilt also the frame lines around the center motif.

Using the machine stitching as a guide, and allowing a ⅜-inch seam allowance outside the stitching, trim the outside edges of the embroidered quilt top in the scallop shape. Trim the batting and backing to the same contour.

Turn the raw edges to the inside and whipstitch the edge to finish.

Quilt ⅜ inch from the edge, following the scallop pattern.

Pull one of the heavy threads in the lace heading to gather the lace edging. Leaving a ½-inch unattached tail for a seam allowance and beginning at the center of the bottom edge, hand-whip the gathered edging to the scalloped edge of the quilt. At the end leave another ½-inch tail. Turn the two tails to the wrong side and seam. A narrow zigzag sewing machine stitch makes a strong seam that can be trimmed along the stitches to make an almost invisible join.

BÉBÉ

A CRIB-SIZE QUILT WITH SHADOW QUILTING
Finished size: 36″ × 50″

THIS QUILT IS DESTINED TO BE AN HEIR-loom. Not only does it look and feel like one, it has a design so delicate that it is bound to be the favorite, treasured and kept for future babies. The use of Swiss batiste lends another dimension to the sense that this is a special quilt, for this fabric is strong as well as beautiful.

Quilting around a layer of color under a sheer white surface adds a subtle dimension to a baby quilt. The stitching holds the colored pieces between the layers and adds at the same time the texture of the quilting itself. Known as shadow quilting, the technique used here is really quite simple, the results intriguing.

Although this design has been finished as a shadow quilting project, it is a versatile design that would also make a very elegant all-white quilt. In addition, the flowers and bows are ideal for a stenciled project. The stenciling could be strong colors placed under the top layer of batiste, as the fabric was in this quilt, or could be in pastels stenciled to the top, as were the hearts on Little Princess on page 102.

Finding the Materials

When choosing fabrics—these can be all-cotton as specified or a blend of fibers—find first the sheer (white) batiste. Then lay the colors for the design under a layer of the sheer batiste to see if the colors will be right when quilted. Generally, the colors needed will be stronger than those first chosen; some simply will not be effective under the white layer. Note also that in the Materials list, the fiber content of the colors has not been specified, since color is the most important feature there and a mixture of fibers will work fine.

There are many transfer adhesives. If you find several, buy just a sample of each and test them to find the one that leaves the fabric most flexible.

Materials

White Swiss batiste, 100% cotton, 42″ wide—5¼ yards
Pink, yellow, rose, and green batiste—4″ × 4″ each color
Blue batiste, 42″ wide—¼ yard
Traditional quilt batting— 38″ × 52″
#50 white cotton mercerized thread for quilting and construction
Iron-on transfer pencil
Iron-on transfer adhesive—½ yard
Cotton cording—5½ yards

See also the notes about fabric for Petite Bébé on page 126.

Before you begin working, check the Basic Sewing Supplies list on page 11 and the Basic Quilting Supplies list on page 12 to make sure you have everything you will need on hand.

Marking

Set one of the white pieces aside for the quilt back. Divide one of the two remaining pieces into quarters by folding it lengthwise, bringing the selvages together, then folding the long piece crosswise to bring the raw edges together. Press in the creases. This is the quilt top facing onto which the quilt pattern will be traced. The colored design pieces will be sandwiched between this and the quilt top, which does not require marking.

Following the instructions for Petite Bébé (page 129) and referring to the drawing of the quilt, trace the border and center motif design for the doll quilt. Take the drawings to a copy shop and enlarge them to 208 percent of the original size. This will make the distance between the slashed repeat lines on the border 7 inches rather than the 3⅜ inches on the drawing. Check for accuracy to make certain the design will fit the fabric. (On most self-service copiers, the greatest enlargement that can be made is 141 percent. For this design, the first copy was 141 percent; then that enlargement was copied at 141 percent. Still not quite full size, the second copy was enlarged to 103 percent to make the distance between the slashed lines on the border exactly 7 inches.)

Use the quilt drawing (left) to mark the quilt top facing, following the instructions for Petite Bébé.

Even though the blue pieces for the shadow quilting design are small and numerous, the use of the iron-on adhesive and a little organization make

Cutting Guide

Cut from the white batiste:
   3 pieces 42 × 54 inches
   Use the remaining ¾ yard to cut 198 inches of 1-inch bias strips for the corded piping.

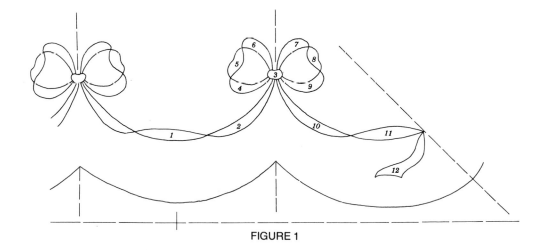

FIGURE 1

placing the colored design elements an easily managed task. One way to accomplish this is to number each section of the design as has been done on the small drawing (Figure 1) of the single bow in the border. Place these numbers on your enlarged drawings of the border.

Using an iron-on transfer pencil, trace the *wrong* side of your drawings and use them as hot-iron transfers. Most pencils will make four or five transfers—each a little bit lighter—before needing reapplication. You will need to make twenty of each numbered piece to complete the border. Make that many copies by ironing the tracing onto the blue fabric.

After transfering the designs onto the blue fabric, iron the transfer adhesive to the other side of the fabric. Next, cut the pieces apart on the transfer lines. The little pieces will separate when the points of the elements are reached. As this happens, drop each onto a paper with a number corresponding to the number assigned the piece in Figure 1.

The best place to work is the ironing board. Set the iron temperature as suggested by the maker of the adhesive. Using both your outline on the batiste and the numbers on the tracing, peel off the paper on the pieces and iron them to the marked facing. Use just a quick touch to fuse the pieces securely in place, then when all are fastened, go over the entire piece and follow the manufacturer's instructions for setting them permanently.

Repeat for the center motif, using the colors shown on the color drawing. You need make only one transfer of each piece for the center. After working on the border, you will probably not need to number the design pieces, but do so if you feel it would be easier.

When placing the fabric for the flowers, put down the pale pink first, then the rose, finally the yellow center, stacking them one on top of the other.

Assembling the Quilt

Place the unmarked quilt top over the facing, with the colored appliqué pieces between the two. Smooth the layers so they are perfectly aligned, and pin them securely together. The scallop lines on the facing should be visible through the batiste. With a straight machine stitch—about eight stitches to the inch on machines that measure stitches per inch, about 1½ mm for newer machines—carefully stitch on the scallop lines to hold the quilt top and facing together.

Make the corded piping following the instructions on page 22. With the raw edges of the piping and the quilt top matching, stitch the piping to the quilt top, following the line of stitching for the scallops. Clip the edges of the piping seam allowance on the curves so the piping will lie flat. Stitch to the points of the scallops; leave the needle down in the fabric and pivot the piece to turn.

Assemble the layers of the quilt, beginning with the backing, adding the batting, and finally the faced top with the right side facing up. Pin securely, then baste, placing the rows of basting about 1 inch apart.

Quilt around all the colored pieces. This is additional fastening for the glued pieces and adds the quilting dimension to the design. In addition, quilt around the frame surrounding the center motif.

Trim all three layers to the scallop shape, allowing a ½-inch seam allowance. Trim the batting an additional ⅛ inch. Turn the raw edges to the inside and fasten with small invisible stitches. As you do this stitching, hold the little extra width of the batting to the inside. It makes a prettier edge if this extra is there.

As a final flourish, quilt ½ inch inside the corded outside edge.

BLUEBIRDS FOR BABY

A STENCILED DOLL QUILT
Finished size: 14¼" × 18¾" exclusive of 1½" lace edging ruffle

Sprightly little bluebirds ent-
wine blue ribbons into bows, and country pinks add a sparkle of color to this little quilt.
Accenting an interesting quilting pattern, entredeux and wide gathered lace add touches that
make this a delightful gift for a special little girl.

Materials
Pale ivory poly-blend batiste,
    42" wide—⅛ yard
Low-loft quilt batting—
    15½" × 20"
#50 ivory cotton mercerized
    quilting thread
White lace edging, 90% cotton,
    1½" wide—5½ yards
White entredeux—2 yards
Stencil paints—blue, rose, green,
    and yellow
Stencil film—8" × 12"
Black fabric marker with fine tip
Washout pen
Masking tape—½"

Finding the Materials
These materials should all be easy to find. Choose a dress- or blouse-weight
batiste that is tightly woven, so the batting fibers won't migrate through.
Since the piece is so small, regular sewing thread in a 50 weight has been used,
so the stitches are small in keeping with the delicacy of the quilt.

Before you begin working, check the Basic Sewing Supplies list on page 11,
the Basic Quilting Supplies list on page 12, and the Stenciling Supplies list on
page 26 to make sure you have everything you will need on hand.

Cutting, Marking, and Stenciling
Wash and iron dry the batiste, then cut it into two pieces 18 × 22½ inches.

Lay out the basic design on one of the pieces of batiste. Following the Layout
Drawing, find the centers of the sides and mark lines A and B by pressing them
in. (This is to avoid ironing over blue lines when the paint is set.) Measuring
out from these lines as indicated on the drawing, mark the 14¼ × 18¾-inch
rectangle with a washout pen. Leave the surplus fabric around the rectangle
until after the quilting is finished.

Cut the stencils, using the black lines on the color drawing as your pattern.
This drawing has been included in color so you can see the way the birds
should be shaded where the rose meets the blue.

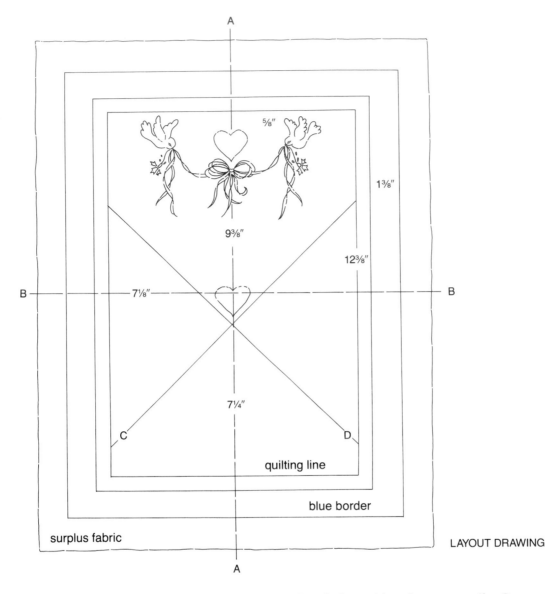

A

5/8"

1 3/8"

9 3/8"

12 3/8"

B —— 7 1/8" —— B

7 1/4"

C   D

quilting line

blue border

surplus fabric   LAYOUT DRAWING

A

You can paint this design with only two stencils. Cut one for all openings marked 1, the second for those marked 2. You can use the same stencils for both sections of the design of the birds and ribbon tendrils if you complete one side, then clean the stencil and turn it over to reverse the image for the other side.

Place the birds on the piece as shown on the Layout Drawing, centering them at the top with the tips of the wings 5/8 inch from the blue border across the top. The knot of the bow should be on line A.

Paint the birds and ribbons, flowers and stems. The two flowers and the birds' breasts should be rose, the stems and leaves green, the birds' beaks yellow, everything else blue. Although you have cut two stencils for the blue ribbons, paint both with the same blue. Using the black fabric marker, draw the birds' eyes, following the picture for placement and shape.

Using a long straightedge cut from cardboard or stencil film, paint the outer border. Instead of making a line to denote the inner edge of the border, measure in from the outside line 1⅜ inches and hold the straightedge in place while painting. Notice in the color photograph that the border has not been painted a solid blue but is darker at the edges, shading almost to white near the middle for an old look.

Set the color as the manufacturer suggests.

With a washout pen, mark a quilting line ½ inch inside the blue border as shown on the Layout Drawing. Measuring along this line from the lower edge of the rectangle, place a dot 12⅜ inches from the bottom.

Measure up from the outside line of the rectangle on line A 7¼ inches and make a dot.

Lay a straightedge through the dot on the quilting line and the dot on the

center line just made, and mark a quilting line through the two, extending the line to the edge as shown by lines C and D on the Layout Drawing.

Using the heart stencil design for the Little Princess Quilt on page 104, cut a template—typing paper will be fine—for the heart.

Trace one heart centered over the bow with the point of the heart about ½ inch above the knot. Trace another heart at the center of the V formed by the crossed quilting lines C and D, placing it ½ inch above the lines.

Assembly

Layer the quilt back, the batting and the stenciled top, smoothing out all wrinkles. Pin the layers together and baste.

Quilt around all the stenciled design, placing the stitches on the background right beside the edges of the color. Quilt on the edge of the blue border as well as on the quilting line ½ inch inside it. Quilt around each heart. Begin the diamond quilting by first stitching lines C and D. Then lay a piece of ½-inch-wide masking tape along each line, and stitch beside it to quilt the ½-inch grid lines that form the diamond pattern.

After all the quilting has been completed, trim all three layers evenly ½ inch beyond the marked edges of the blue border. Trim the batting another ¼ inch. Turn the raw edges of the quilt top and the backing to the inside, tucking in the batting, and whipstitch them closed.

Trim the batiste edge from one side of the entredeux and whipstitch the trimmed edge to the outside edges of the quilt.

Pull one of the heavy threads in the heading of the lace to gather it to fit the outside of the quilt. Trim the remaining batiste from the entredeux, and whipstitch the gathered lace to it.

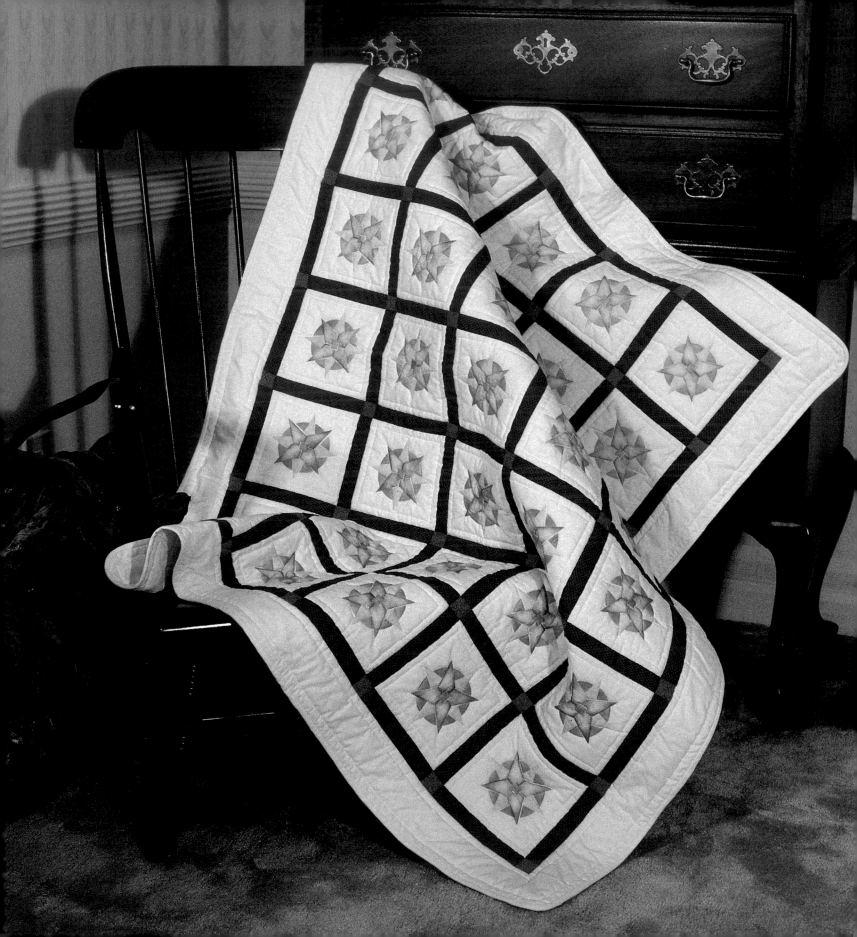

LITTLE MARINER

A STENCILED SNUGGLER
Finished size: 42″ × 55″

Quilters have loved stenciling since Colonial days, appreciating the ease of painting a design that would take much time if embroidered or appliquéd. Thus the thirty-five squares for this little "antique" can easily be stenciled in an evening and assembled ready to quilt in a few additional hours. Antiquing with a coffee or tea solution would add an even more authentic look.

Materials

Ivory muslin, 100% cotton,
 42″ wide—3¼ yards
Deep blue geometric print, 100%
 cotton, 42″ wide—¾ yard
Red geometric print, 100% cotton,
 42″ wide—¼ yard
Traditional polyester quilt
 batting—crib size
Stencil film—13″ × 13″
Stencil crayons—red, gold,
 and blue
#50 off-white cotton mercerized
 machine sewing thread for
 construction
Quilting thread—transparent
 nylon for machine, or off-white
 cotton for hand quilting

Finding the Materials

Look for a smooth-finish cotton for the background so the stenciling will have sharp edges. The list calls for ivory—just another way of saying off-white. Choose the stencil crayons and the small prints together, so they match. The stencil crayons used for the photographed quilt were named Cinnamon Stick, Chamois Yellow, and Cobalt Blue by the manufacturer. The blue is a true cobalt, the yellow is deep with a soft gold effect, the red is very rusty. The overall coloring lends a soft Colonial look.

If you are unable to obtain stencil crayons, or if you prefer fabric paint, look for similar colors and follow the manufacturer's instructions for application and setting the color.

Before you begin working, check the Basic Sewing Supplies list on page 11, the Basic Quilting Supplies list on page 12, and the Stenciling Supplies list on page 26 to make sure you have everything you will need on hand.

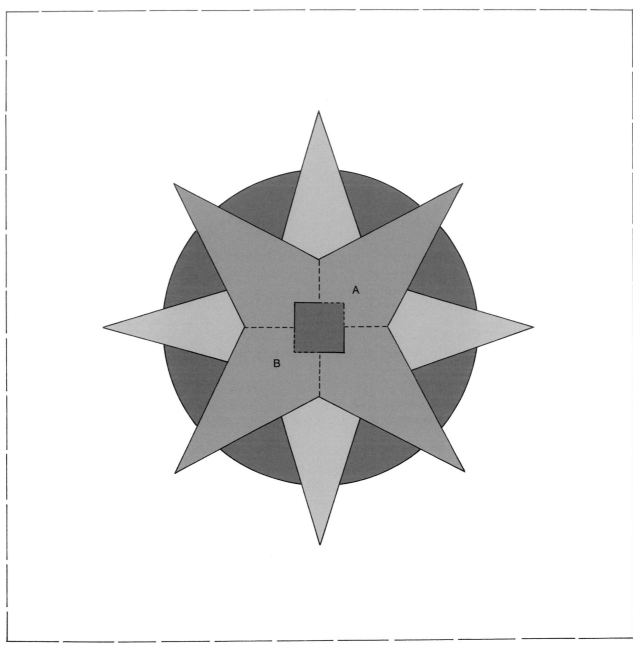

FIGURE 1

Stenciling the Squares

If stenciling on fabric is a new technique for you, please read the basic instructions on page 26 before beginning.

Three stencils are necessary for this design. Using the outline of the square for Figure 1, cut three 6½-inch squares from the stencil film. When tracing, match the edges of the film squares to the outline of the square in Figure 1 and all the cutouts will automatically be centered. Onto one square, trace only the areas colored red. On the second, trace the yellow portions of the design. On the third, trace just the two blue star points marked A and B. Use the tiny dotted line around the red square so your tracing looks like Figure 2. (Yours will be the same size as your other tracing. Figure 2 has been reduced.)

Cut out the three stencils. Using the edges of the stencil as a guide for centering the design, stencil the thirty-five ivory squares. Color the red areas first. Next place the blue stencil and color the two points. Rotate the stencil to paint the remaining two points. Finish by coloring the yellow sections. Set the paint as recommended by the manufacturer.

Assembling the Quilt Top

Beginning and ending with a blue lattice strip, stitch five stenciled squares and six blue strips into a row. Repeat to complete seven rows. Trim the seams and press.

Cutting Guide

From the ivory cut:
  The quilt backing, 42 × 55 inches (If your fabric is a little wider, just leave the extra width until you trim for the bias binding.)
  Enough 1½-inch bias strips to piece into a 198-inch strip
  35 squares 6½ × 6½ inches
  2 pieces 3½ × 49 inches
  2 pieces 3½ × 42 inches
From the blue print cut:
  80 lattice strips 1½ × 6½ inches
From the red print cut:
  48 squares 1½ × 1½ inches

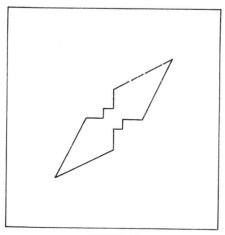

FIGURE 2

Beginning and ending with a red square, stitch six red squares and five blue lattice strips together end to end. Repeat to make eight strips. Trim the seams and press.

Join the rows of squares and the narrow lattice strips, beginning and ending with the lattice strips. Match the seams carefully so they all line up. Trim the seams and press. The completed pieced section should measure 36×49 inches.

Stitch the two 49-inch ivory border pieces to the 49-inch sides. Trim the seams and press them toward the blue. Repeat, stitching the two 42-inch strips to the top and bottom.

Finishing the Quilt

Lay the ivory backing on a flat surface, wrong side up. Place the batting on top, smoothing out any extra fullness. Finish with the quilt top, right side up. Pin the layers together securely. If you intend to machine-quilt, use safety pins to avoid basting. For hand quilting, baste the layers together, placing the rows of stitches about 1½ inches apart.

Quilt "in the ditch" along all seam lines. Outline-quilt around the stenciled areas, placing the stitching on the background fabric at the edges of the color. Also quilt ½ inch inside the outline of each square and ½ inch outside the blue outlining the pieced field. (This amounts to quilting on every line on the quilt drawing except the one indicating the bias binding on the outside.)

Trim the edges evenly. Following the instructions for bias binding on page 23, finish the edges with the ivory binding. If you like, another row of quilting ½ inch inside the bias binding may be added.

BLUE AND WHITE BOW TIES

A COUNTRY-STYLE PIECED DOLL QUILT

Finished size: 20″ × 24½″

ONE OF THE GREATEST DELIGHTS OF patchwork is the many ways one pattern can be varied either by changing colors or the way the squares themselves are set. Of course, this often means that before one quilt is complete, several others are already designed and ready to be put together. The Bow Tie patchwork pattern is an old favorite that starts one on this road. Just a small variation in color, background, or set creates another new pattern.

For this sprightly little doll quilt, the Bow Ties themselves are white, with the squares set diagonally on the blue background to accent the contrasting ties. The bold checked border is a wonderful counterpoint to the Bow Tie design, completing a quilt any doll would be proud to call her own.

Although the 2-inch size of the finished blocks is smaller than those usually used for a bed-size quilt, these are large enough to be easy to handle and to piece. Machine piecing and quilting make this a quick little project, but one with cheerful country results that will be treasured.

Materials

Blue floral calico print, 100% cotton, 42″ wide—1¼ yards

White muslin, 100% cotton, 42″ wide—1 yard

Traditional quilt batting— 23″ × 27″

Quilting thread—either matching blue cotton or transparent nylon

Finding the Materials

Although the blue and white color scheme is beloved, almost any color paired with white or off-white would work beautifully in the design. The specified cotton materials are lovely, but you could also do well with a blended fabric. It would also be fun to make this quilt in crib size.

Before you begin working, check the Basic Sewing Supplies list on page 11 and the Basic Quilting Supplies list on page 12 to make sure you have everything you will need on hand.

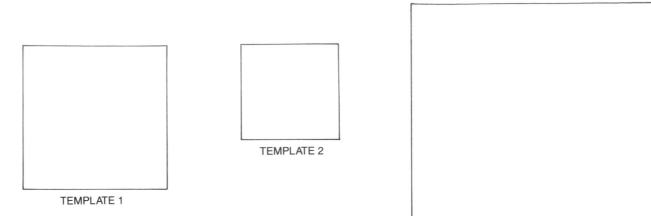

TEMPLATE 1

TEMPLATE 2

TEMPLATE 3

Cutting Guide

Cut from the blue fabric:
   The quilt backing, 23 × 27
   inches
   70 squares 1½ × 1½ inches
   (Template 1)
   54 squares 2½ × 2½ inches
   (Template 3)
   2 strips 1¼ × 20 inches
   7 strips 1½ × 45 inches
Cut from the white muslin:
   70 squares 1½ × 1½ inches
   (Template 1)
   70 squares 1 × 1 inches
   (Template 2)
   7 strips 1½ × 45 inches
   2 strips 1 × 24½ inches
   2 strips 1 × 29 inches
   Enough 1-inch-wide bias strips
   to make 100 inches

Assembling the Squares

One complete square as drawn requires: two white 1½-inch squares (Template 1), two blue 1½-inch squares (Template 1), and two white 1-inch squares (Template 2).

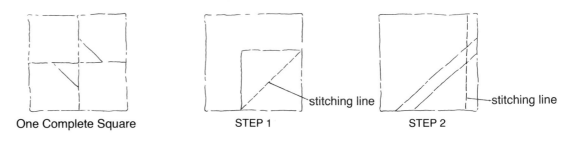

One Complete Square   STEP 1   STEP 2

To Make One Square

With right sides together, stitch a small white square to a blue square, holding the pieces as shown in Step 1. Trim the seam to ⅛ inch and press. Make two.

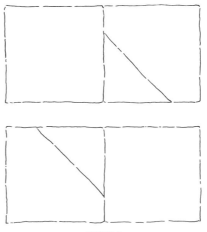

STEP 3

QUILTING GUIDE

Quilt "in the ditch" on every line except the two lines denoting bias binding. Also, quilt inside each blue calico square as shown by the small dashed stitching lines.

Holding the pieces as shown in the drawing for Step 2, stitch the pieced square just made to a plain white square—this white piece is underneath the pieced square in the drawing. Trim the seam and press. Make two.

Lay the two pieces in position as shown in Step 3. With right sides together, stitch them together along the line A-B, making a ¼-inch seam allowance. Trim the seam and press. The finished square measures 2½ inches on each side.

Following this procedure, complete thirty-five squares.

Assembling the Quilt Top

A quick and practical assembly method for little quilts uses full squares that are later trimmed to shape instead of a combination of squares and triangles to join the pieced squares into a rectangular field.

Figure 1, Assembling the Pieced Field, shows the way the 2½-inch blue squares are attached to the Bow Tie squares. Begin with Row 1 at the top left of the drawing. This is just a single blue square. Note the way Row 2 increases to three squares—one Bow Tie and two plain blue calico. Row 3 consists of five squares, and so on for the remaining rows.

Assemble the fourteen rows as shown. Trim the seams and press. Lay the stitched rows on a flat surface in the same order as the drawing.

Beginning with Rows 1 and 2, stitch the rows together. Trim the seams and press.

Place the piece on the cutting mat; line up the ruler with the points at which the seam allowances meet—¼ inch from the points of the bow on the sides—and cut off the excess points to make a rectangle 14½ × 20 inches. (See cutting lines on Figure 1.)

Stitch the two 1¼ × 20-inch blue strips to the long sides of the pieced top, taking care to stitch so the seam is right at the tips of the white points. Trim the seam and press. (These two strips make the distance from the white points to the edge at the sides equal to that at the top and bottom.)

Assembling the Checked Border

The finished field measures 15¼ × 20 inches. Set it aside and make the checked borders next.

Stitch together two sets of 1½ × 45-inch strips. For one, begin with blue and alternate with white, ending with blue as in Figure 2. For the other, begin with white and alternate with blue, ending with white as in Figure 3. Trim all seams to ¼ inch and press.

row 1
row 2
row 3

cutting line

cutting line

FIGURE 1

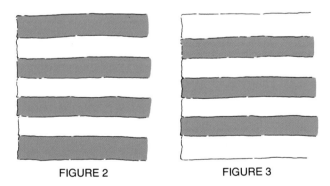

FIGURE 2   FIGURE 3

Cut the long striped pieces across the seams into 1½-inch pieces. Match one strip beginning with white to one beginning with blue and stitch them together. Trim the seam and press. You now have a 7½-inch piece of checked border that looks like Figure 4. Repeat with the other pieces.

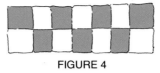

FIGURE 4

Join the short border pieces into lengths 9 inches longer than the sides of the pieced top. Two strips should be 24¼ inches long; two should be 29 inches. Stitch a strip of the 1-inch-wide white muslin to each strip so you have two rows of alternating blue and white squares with a white border at the top, as in Figure 5.

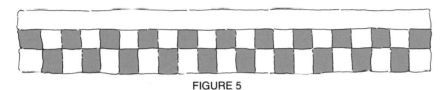

FIGURE 5

With right sides together, stitch the white edges of the border pieces to the four sides of the quilt. Begin and end the stitching ¼ inch from the ends. Leave the surplus border lengths hanging free. Trim the seams and press.

Lay the quilt top on the ironing board with the right side up. Turn one free end of the border to the wrong side, making a right angle as shown in Figure 6. Lay a right triangle along the fold as shown in the drawing to ascertain the angle is true. Press in the fold. Turn the other border end to the wrong side and adjust the fold so it meets the pressed side. Turn the top over and pin the two fold lines together. Stitch exactly on the fold lines. Trim off the excess border and press. (Technically, the miter should cut across the blue and white pattern as shown on the quilt drawing, but chances are it will be slightly different, though still pretty.)

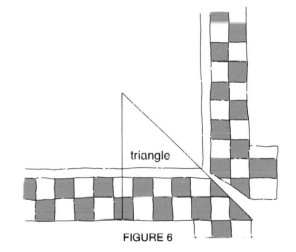

triangle

FIGURE 6

Finishing

Layer the quilt back, the batting, and the pieced top, smoothing out all wrinkles. Pin the layers together securely. Baste.

The Quilting Guide (page 153) shows one corner of the quilt. Machine-quilt with either blue or transparent thread "in the ditch," outlining all the squares. Outline all the Bow Ties and quilt ¼ inch from the seam inside each blue square as noted on the Quilting Guide. Note on the Quilting Guide that the crossed lines in the knot are not shown. These need not be quilted.

When all quilting has been completed, trim away excess batting and backing. Bind the edges with the white bias, following the instructions on page 23.

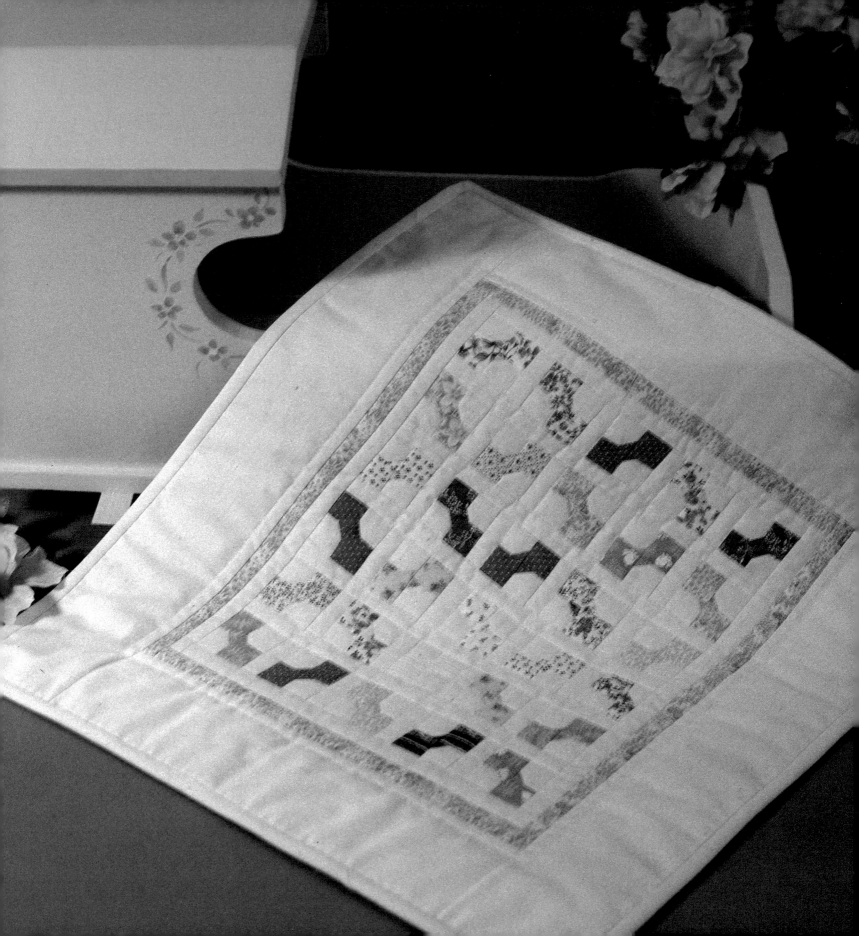

TINY BOW TIES

A MINIATURE PIECED DOLL QUILT
Finished size: 15¼" × 17¼"

MADE FROM LEFTOVER PIECES OF A LIT-tle girl's clothing, this miniature scrap quilt made for a doll can be a reminder of many happy hours spent sewing for the special occasions that make family memories special. One little Bow Tie might be from the special dress for the very first day of school, another a tiny piece of sweet rompers, another part of a favorite shirt. All bring out smiles and make the stitching fun!

If you have not yet tried a reduced-size patchwork design, this Bow Tie is a good one with which to experiment. It is small enough to be appropriate for a doll, but not so tiny as to be difficult to handle.

Materials

15 assorted 100% cotton print pieces—each 5" × 2⅛"
One print for the inside border—2" × 42"
Unbleached muslin, 100% cotton, 42" wide—¾ yard
Low-loft quilt batting—18" × 20"
#50 off-white cotton mercerized thread for quilting and construction

Finding the Materials

Each 5 × 2⅛-inch rectangle will make the printed sections for two Bow Tie squares. Since the pieces are small, choose fabrics that will not fray easily. If you are working with little pieces from your scrap collection, you can mix both blends and all-cotton with no problem.

Before you begin working, check the Basic Sewing Supplies list on page 11 and the Basic Quilting Supplies list on page 12 to make sure you have everything you will need on hand.

157

Cutting Guide

Cut from each 5 × 2⅛-inch print
piece:
  4 squares 1¼ × 1¼ inches
  (Template 1)
  4 squares ⅞ × ⅞ inches
  (Template 2)
Cut from the border print:
  2 strips 1 × 10½ inches
  2 strips 1 × 13½ inches
Cut from the muslin:
  The quilt backing, 18 × 20
  inches
  60 squares 1¼ × 1¼ inches
  (Template 1)
  20 lattice strips 1 × 2 inches
  7 horizontal lattice strips
  1 × 9½ inches
  2 vertical frame pieces 1 × 12½
  inches
  2 border pieces 3 × 11½ inches
  2 border pieces 3 × 19½ inches
  Enough 1-inch-wide bias strips
  to make 78 inches

Assembling the Squares

One complete square as drawn on page 152 requires two muslin squares (Template 1), two print squares (Template 1), and two print squares (Template 2).

To Make One Square

With right sides together, stitch a small print square to a muslin square, holding the pieces as shown in Step 1 on page 152. Trim the seam to ⅛ inch and press. Make two.

TEMPLATE 1   TEMPLATE 2

Holding the pieces as shown in the drawing for Step 2 on page 152, stitch the pieced square to a print one—the print one is underneath the pieced square in the drawing. Trim the seam and press. Make two.

Lay the pieces in position as shown in Step 3 on page 152. With right sides together, stitch them together along line A-B making a ¼-inch seam allowance. Trim the seam to ⅛ inch and press. The finished square measures 2 inches on both side.

Following this method, make thirty squares.

Assembling the Quilt Top

Lay the little squares on a flat surface and arrange them in six horizontal rows of five squares each, taking into consideration distribution of color and the angle of the bows themselves. On the pictured quilt, the slant of the bows alternates across the rows. It would be just as attractive if all slanted in the same direction as for the Blue and White Bow Ties quilt, page 150. Try both arrangements and choose the prettiest.

Join the squares into six horizontal rows by stitching the 1 × 2-inch lattice strips to the sides of the squares. Begin and end the rows with Bow Tie squares. Trim the seams; press.

Join the six horizontal rows with five 1 × 9½-inch horizontal lattice strips. Use the two remaining horizontal lattice strips at the top and bottom of the piece. Trim the seams. Press.

Stitch the two muslin 1 × 12½-inch vertical frame pieces to the sides. Trim the seams. Press.

Stitch the 10½-inch print border pieces to the top and bottom of the piece. Trim the seams. Press. Stitch the remaining two border pieces to the sides. Trim the seam and press.

Add the muslin outer border, stitching the 11½-inch pieces to the top and bottom first, then adding the longer side pieces. Trim the seams and press. The finished quilt top should measure 17½ × 19 inches. Press it well.

Finishing

Layer the muslin quilt backing, the batting, and the quilt top, smoothing out any wrinkles. Pin the layers together and baste. Machine-quilt "in the ditch" on all seams. Add another row of quilting on the muslin border ¼ inch outside the seam of the print border.

When the quilting has been completed, bind the edges with the muslin bias pieces, following the instructions on page 23.

IRISH LULLABY

A BELOVED CLASSIC FOR THE NURSERY
Finished size: 40″ × 48″

THERE IS A GRAPHIC SIMPLICITY THAT lends great beauty to this old design and makes it one of the most loved of all time. Although it is lovely in other colors—even in small prints—the blue and white coloring is the most dear. Reduced in scale, this version of the Single Irish Chain pattern is perfect for the nursery of either a baby boy or a little girl. It will blend or mix with other patterns, adding its own geometric elegance and cuddly softness.

The instructions below give two alternative methods for constructing the blocks: one at a time, and quick assembly for all twenty. The Cutting Guide lists all the pieces needed for the quick assembly method for all twenty blocks.

Materials
White 100% cotton, 42″ wide—
 3 yards
Pale blue 100% cotton, 42″
 wide—¾ yards
Pale blue print, 100% cotton, 42″
 wide—1½ yards
#50 white cotton mercerized
 thread for quilting and
 construction
Traditional quilt batting—crib size

Finding the Materials
Look for a pale chambraylike blue to give the quilt a delicate coloring or a crisp deep blue for a very contemporary feel. Both blue and white fabrics should be tightly woven. This quilt has been finished with a blue background backing printed with a small randomly scattered white alphabet. Any small print can be substituted or the blue from the top could be used. The yardages for the two have been separated in the Materials list for your choice.

The traditional quilt batting allows for small hand quilting stitches or easy machine quilting.

Before you begin working, check the Basic Sewing Supplies list on page 11 and the Basic Quilting Supplies list on page 12 to make sure you have everything you will need on hand.

Cutting Guide

From the white cotton cut:

Bias strips 1½ inches wide to total 5 yards for the outside binding

6 strips 1½ × 42 inches for the Four-Patch corner units

4 strips 1½ × 42 inches for the Nine-Patch units

80 rectangles 2½ × 3½ inches

49 pieces 1½ × 7 inches for sashing

2 pieces 4 × 32½ inches for border

2 pieces 4 × 48½ inches for border

From the blue cotton cut:

6 strips 1½ × 42 inches for the Four-Patch corner units

5 strips 1½ × 42 inches for the Nine-Patch units

30 squares 1½ × 1½ inches for sashing blocks

From the blue print cut:

The quilt backing, 41 × 49 inches

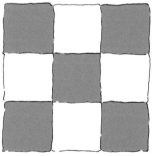

FIGURE 3

FIGURE 4

162

To Assemble One Block

Figure 1 shows one complete block. The complete quilt contains twenty of these blocks.

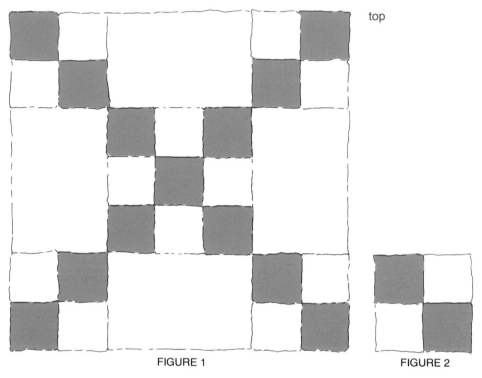

top

FIGURE 1

FIGURE 2

Each block is composed of three basic parts. Notice the four corner units which are Four-Patch squares (Figure 2). The center is a Nine-Patch square (Figure 3). The voids are filled with white rectangles.

Four-Patch Corner Units

The four corner units of one block can be made from 12 inches of each of the 1½ × 42-inch white and blue strips listed in the Cutting Guide. Using an accurate ¼-inch seam, stitch a blue strip to a white strip along the 12-inch side. Trim the seam to ⅛″ and press it flat, but do not press it open. Measure along the seam and cut the strip into 1½-inch lengths. Press the pieces open, pressing the seams toward the blue.

Holding two pieces with right sides together and placing the colors as shown in Figure 4, stitch a ¼-inch seam to complete a corner unit. Trim the seam to ⅛ inch and press to one side. Make three more corners.

The Nine-Patch Center Unit

To construct a center Nine-Patch unit, again use the 1½-inch wide strips of blue and white. Stitch these together to make three pieces like those shown in

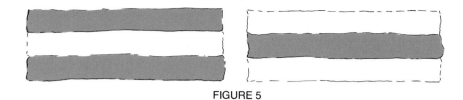

FIGURE 5

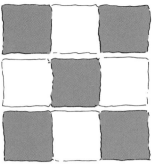

FIGURE 6

Figure 5. Two should alternate blue, white, blue. One strip should alternate white, blue, white. Measure along the seam line and cut the strips into 1½-inch lengths.

Positioning the three pieces and distributing the colors as shown in Figure 6, stitch them together to make a completed Nine-Patch like the one shown in Figure 3. Trim and press the seams.

To Complete the Block

Cut four white pieces 2½ × 3½ inches. Lay out the four corner units, the center Nine-Patch unit, and the four white rectangles as shown in Figure 7. Stitch the white rectangles to the corner squares for the top and bottom rows first. Next stitch the white to the sides of the center unit. Finally, stitch the three rows together. Carefully trim seams and press. The finished block should measure 7 × 7 inches.

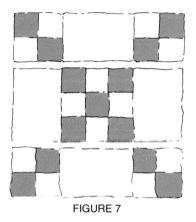

FIGURE 7

Quick Assembly Method to Make Twenty Blocks

Step 1: Cut all pieces listed on the Cutting Guide. Keep them sorted and note the designation of each group of pieces.

Step 2: Stitch the six white and the six blue 1½ × 42-inch strips together in pairs, one of each color, along the 42-inch sides to make six blue-white pieces. Press and trim the seams. Cut these into 1½-inch pieces as for the Four-Patch corner units, *above*. Seam them together to make eighty corner units.

Step 3: Seam together the remaining blue and the remaining white 1½-inch-wide strips to create two pieces that alternate blue, white, blue, and one that alternates white, blue, white, as shown if Figure 5.

Trim the seams and press well. Cut these into 1½-inch-wide pieces. There should be twenty of the white-blue-white pieces, forty of the blue-white-blue pieces.

Following the directions for the Nine-Patch center unit, *above*, construct twenty of those pieces. Trim and press as before.

Step 4: Following the instructions To Complete the Block, *above*, finish constructing the twenty blocks.

Assembling the Quilt Top

Step 1: Lay the completed squares out on a flat surface in five rows of four blocks each.

Step 2: Beginning and ending with a 7-inch sashing strip and alternating blocks with sashing strips, sew the horizontal rows together. Trim and press the seams.

Step 3: Beginning and ending with a blue block, stitch four sashing strip and five blue blocks into six strips.

Step 4: Beginning and ending with the long, narrow blue and white sashing pieces made in Step 3, join the five rows of blocks together. Trim and press the seams.

Step 5: Stitch the $4 \times 32\frac{1}{2}$-inch white border pieces to the top and bottom of the quilt. Press the seams and trim. Stitch the $49\frac{1}{2}$-inch borders to the sides. Press the seams and trim.

Step 6: Make a tracing of the border quilting pattern (Figure 8) using a pen that makes a line heavy enough to be visible through the white fabric. Place

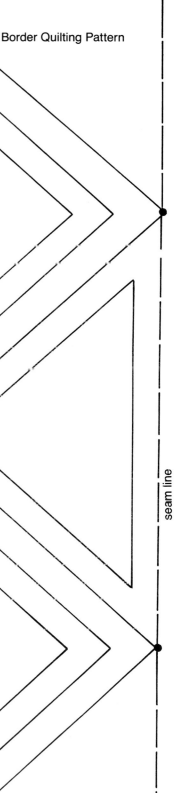

Border Quilting Pattern

seam line

the tracing under the white border with a large dot at the center of the side and mark the quilting lines out toward the ends, repeating between the dots. Place the dots at the seam line as shown on the pattern. If there is any differences in the size of your quilt top, your corners may be slightly different from those shown in the drawing of the quilt, but should work our nicely.

Step 7: Layer the quilt backing, the batting, and the complete top, smoothing out all wrinkles. Pin and baste the layers together.

Step 8: Using the #50 white cotton thread, quilt by hand or machine following the Quilting Guide for placement of stitches.

Step 9: Using the bias pieces and following the instructions on page 23, finish the edges with white bias binding. Stitch the binding so the points of the quilted border just touch the seam line as on the Quilting Guide.

FIGURE 8   165

A Final Flourish—Your Signature

A little touch that adds much to a quilt is your signature and the date penned or embroidered on a corner of the back. You can make a little label and sew it on or you can embroider a corner of the backing fabric.

The most personal and permanent notation is written in your own script, then embroidered in small stitches before the quilt is finished. The message can vary in many ways. You can be formal and include a lot of information as I did for Nicole on a quilt I hoped she would keep a long time (Figure 1). You might want to simply sign your name and the date, or you could add "I love you" to your name as I did for Baby Barry (Figure 2), thinking that the quilt I was making might possibly be her choice as a security blanket.

Decide what you want to say, then think about embroidery or ink as a medium. If you choose ink, a separate label is a good idea since it is difficult to predict how the ink will affect the fibers of the fabric after a long period of time. Cut a piece of fabric larger than you think you will need. Iron it. Then, using a fine-point, nonbleeding fabric pen, write your message. Cut to size allowing for borders to turn under on all four sides, then whipstitch it to the quilt with tiny invisible stitches.

If you opt for embroidery, starch the part of the backing onto which you wish to write. Use a #3 pencil with a sharp point and write directly on the fabric. Then embroider the lettering with a single strand of embroidery floss using an embroidery stitch that is easy to work on the tight curves of the writing. I like to use the backstitch or the outline stitch for this. If you wish the notation to be very subtle, use thread that matches the fabric. Thread that contrasts with the color of the fabric will make the message more prominent.

If any pencil shows after the embroidery has been finished, wash out just the embroidered corner. The pencil lines, which are on top of the starch, will disappear as the starch dissolves. Press from the wrong side to dry the fabric.

Baby Barry
I Love You
Mumsie
1993

FIGURE 2

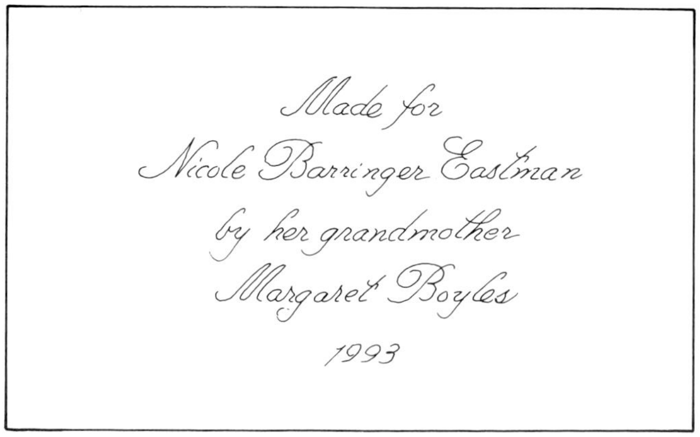

Made for
Nicole Barringer Eastman
by her grandmother
Margaret Boyles
1993

FIGURE 1

Script for Quilts

A B C D E F G H

I J K L M N O P Q R

S T U V W X Y Z

a b c d e f g h i j

k l m n o p q r s t u

v w x y z

1 2 3 4 5 6 7 8 9 0

INDEX

We Care!
All of us at Meredith® Books are dedicated to offering you quality craft books. We welcome your comments and suggestions. Please address correspondence to: Customer Service Department, Meredith® Press, Meredith Corporation, 150 East 52nd Street, New York, NY 10022, or call 1-800-678-2665.